D0444870

Sharing A Laugh

Published by

THOMAS NELSON

Since 1798

www.thomasnelson.com

Copyright © 2007 by Thomas Nelson, Inc.

All rights reserved. No portion of this book may be reproduced, stored in a retrieval system, or transmitted in any form or by any means—electronic, mechanical, photocopy, recording, scanning, or any other—except for brief quotations in critical reviews or articles, without the prior written permission of the publisher.

Published in Nashville, Tennessee by Thomas Nelson, Inc.

Thomas Nelson, Inc. titles may be purchased in bulk for educational, business, fundraising, or sales promotional use. For information, please e-mail SpecialMarkets@ThomasNelson.com.

Compiled and edited by Sue Ann Jones

Some material reprinted from previously published volumes may have been edited slightly from the original.

Unless otherwise noted, Scripture quotations are from The Holy Bible: New International Version® (NIV). Copyright © 1973, 1978, 1984 International Bible Society. Used by permission of Zondervan Bible Publishers. Other Scripture quotations are from the following sources: The Authorized King James Version (KJV). The Living Bible (TLB), copyright © 1971 by Tyndale House Publishers, Wheaton, Ill. Used by permission. The Message (MSG), copyright © 1993. Used by permission of NavPress Publishing Group. The New Century Version (NCV). Copyright © 1987, 1988, 1991 by Word Publishing, a Division of Thomas Nelson, Inc. Used by permission. All rights reserved. The New King James Version® (NKJV). Copyright © 1979, 1980, 1982, Thomas Nelson, Inc., Publishers. The Holy Bible, New Living Translation (NLT). Copyright © 1996 by Tyndale Charitable Trust. Used by permission of Tyndale House Publishers, Wheaton, IL.

Library of Congress Cataloging-in-Publication Data

Sharing a laugh / compiled and edited by Sue Ann Jones.
   p. cm.
   ISBN 10: 0-8499-1866-9
   ISBN 13: 978-0-8499-1866-7
   1. Christian women—Religious life—Humor. I. Jones, Sue Ann.
   BV4527.S4219 2007
   242'.6430207—dc22   2006038729

The best days are filled with laughter.
The very *best days are filled with laughter, shared.*

Contents

Part 3 • *Is This Funny, or Am I Losing My Mind?*
Trying to Remember Why We're Laughing

Part 4 • *Family Funnies*
Laughing with Our Loved Ones

Part 5 • *Healthy Hilarity*
Laughing Is Merry Medicine

Part 6 • *Get Outta Here!*
Laughing at Life's Ridiculous Moments

Part 1

Can You Believe I Did That?

Laughing at Ourselves . . . with Others

• • • • •

You grow up the day you have your
first real laugh—at yourself.
—Ethel Barrymore

Tea Time and Supper

● ● ● Marilyn Meberg

Laughter and bread go together.
—Ecclesiastes 10:19 MSG

I had said, "Never in a million years will I move from Palm Desert, California, to Frisco, Texas." With typical regional arrogance, I believed California to be the only place on earth worthy of loyalty and affection.

So why did I sell my condo in Palm Desert and buy a house in Frisco? Well, here's what seems to have happened. My friend Ney Bailey was driving me around Frisco one morning in search of a good spot for a photo shoot the next day. The photographer wanted an outdoor scene with trees. I've lived in an apartment in Frisco for a few months each year simply because flying from Dallas during our heavy travel season is easier than flying out of Palm Springs, but in those years I didn't ever remember seeing trees. For that matter, I had not seen any hills either, but we apparently didn't need a hill. Ney knew where there were some trees.

We settled on the spot for the photo-shoot but as we were driving away, I saw a house. It beckoned to me. It didn't have any trees, but it was on a lake. The lake is lovely and only a stone's throw from Luci Swindoll's new house. It's four doors down from Nicole Johnson, a three-minute walk from Mary Graham, and a five-minute drive from Sheila and Barry

Walsh. I bought the house and moved into treeless Frisco on December 18, 2004. Mercy!

What a wonder all this is. What draws me to do what I said I'd never do is not only God's relentless pushing and pulling but my love of community. My community is fast congregating in Frisco. God seems to think I need to be there. I like that about Him. I didn't put that plan into motion; He did.

Why is community so important to me? I'm sure it's because I'm an only child. I am energized by the presence of people. Growing up in somewhat isolated and rural communities, I didn't always find a sufficient number of people around. Thank goodness for Mrs. Dunbar.

Mrs. Dunbar was a short bike's ride from my house in Amboy, Washington. We had a weekly tea time at three o'clock each Tuesday. I loved visiting with her because she made the best cookies I've tasted in my short 206 years on this earth. Each Tuesday she made a different cookie for our tea times. When I'd walk into her old rambling house across the street from Wires Cleaners, I'd nearly faint from the glorious smell of just-out-of-the-oven cookies. But not only did I love her cookies, one of her favorite activities in life was to laugh. We made a great pair because it's one of my favorite activities as well.

Mrs. Dunbar had an ill-fitting pair of false teeth that clicked when she talked. She would put me in hysterics by sliding the bottom teeth out of her mouth as far as she could. The goal was to keep them from falling to the floor before she managed to lift them high enough to touch the end of her nose. When she succeeded, we rewarded ourselves with another cookie. By the way, it was considered cheating to use her hands to help the teeth touch the end of her nose.

I was devastated when Mrs. Dunbar died suddenly of an

apparent heart attack. Her son told my father how peaceful she looked lying in bed when he found her. Everything was in order: glasses on top of her Bible, aspirin bottle on the night stand beside her teeth in a glass. I knew it would sound weird if I asked permission to have her teeth, so I kept my mouth shut. But the memory of her laughter and the sight of her teeth meant the world to me. I'd love to live in a community full of Mrs. Dunbars.

The Russian writer Aleksandr Solzhenitsyn said, "It is not the level of prosperity that makes for happiness but the kinship of heart to heart and the way we look at the world that knits us together." Those are my requirements for a successful community. Amy Cella, Nicole Johnson's assistant, is also in this community. She not only meets the requirements, but she, too, is only minutes away from the rest of us. There is a special kinship of heart between us.

Last Sunday some of the community had brunch together after church. I turned to Amy and asked, "What's the best thing that happened to you this week?"

Without the slightest hesitation she said, "I bought a cow." That was one of those delicious fork-dropping moments.

"You what?" nearly everyone chorused. I was envisioning PetSmart and wondering how such a purchase could be made.

Sheila, who was absolutely incredulous, said, "Why? Why would you want to buy a cow?"

I was still lost in PetSmart.

"I bought the cow for food," Amy said.

Still unable to fathom this action, Sheila said, "Are you that sick of grocery shopping? You know our new Kroger is a nice store—it's only two minutes from your house."

"No, that's not the problem," Amy persisted. "I just want

to raise my own beef. I'll feed it only the best 'cow food' and be sure it gets superior care."

Patsy warned Amy about getting attached to the cow.

Sheila suggested not giving the cow a name to restrict possible bonding.

"Oh, I've already named the cow," Amy said. "I'm going to call it Supper. Then after it's grown I can invite people for Supper."

I did one of my spontaneous and obnoxious hoot laughs; there was no getting me under control, in spite of the many disapproving looks I got. That laugh was as hearty as those inspired by Mrs. Dunbar's touch-the-nose-with-the-bottom-teeth trick.

Actually, as I thought about it, I fully understood what Amy is doing. She is raising her recently purchased Supper on a ranch about fifteen minutes from here. We used to do the same thing in the Amboy days. Dad would buy a beef cow, raise it on Harry Hooper's farm, and then off to slaughter it went. We would then stop by Boehm's Deep Freeze every few days and bring home supper. I remember hating it, though. I had named one of the suppers Molly and felt tremendously disloyal as I looked at her on my plate.

Recently I read a newspaper account of a ninety-one-year-old woman who was enthusiastically joining neighborhood friends for a slumber party. The party was from 7 p.m. to 10 p.m. They came in robes, pajamas, and slippers and left whenever they got tired. I can see that happening some thirty years from now in Frisco. I love the notion of being with my dear community right up until the time of slumber parties.

It was Plato who said, "Let me tell you, the more the pleasures of the body fade away, the greater to me is the pleasure and charm of conversations." The only pleasure Plato failed to mention that so characterizes my community is laughter. We will always have conversation . . . we will always have laughter. What a joy!

. . . .

—*Contagious Joy*

Fashion Non-Sense

● ● ● Martha Bolton

*W*hy do we do it to ourselves? Generation after generation of women have willingly exposed themselves to the high risk of pantyhose strangulation, girdle-induced respiratory arrest, and turtleneck tracheotomies. What kind of sick people punish themselves like this?

Even men, for some unknown reason, are into some forms of fashion self-punishment. If you don't believe me, just look at the necktie. Who came up with that idea? Did some fashion designer from the Wild West watch a hanging one day and say, "Now, there's a look that could really catch on"?

Some otherwise intelligent, levelheaded women have sentenced themselves to a lifetime of girdle incarceration. Every morning they insist on squeezing their bodies into those torture devices, one layer at a time. Once it's past the knees, the real tug of war begins. Up a little on the right, up a little on the left. If they're not careful, they can lose their balance and end up doing a little ballet across the room. Actually, it might be more like an opera when you consider the high notes they'll hit every time one of the metal stays pokes them in the ribs.

I've done it myself, and it leaves me asking one simple question—why? Why do we as thinking human beings do these incredibly punishing things to our bodies?

The most torturous of all has got to be pantyhose. Frankly,

I can't imagine how the patent office ever approved the original application for this stuff.

"A nylon half-body suit that fits like a tourniquet but gradually loosens throughout the day until it falls in folds at the ankle like ribbon candy. And it comes in colors. Patent granted. Women'll love it!"

Spandex punishes both sexes. And in some cases, it punishes the onlooker, too. It takes a certain physique to be able to wear spandex, and many of the people we see wearing it these days have seriously violated the Spandex Rules of Engagement.

Sweats, on the other hand, are our reward for having endured decades of fashion abuse. Sweats are comfortable. Roomy. And forgiving. They keep us warm in the winter and cool in the summer. They come in a multitude of colors, and while they don't look that great with high heels and pearls, they do fit in on most occasions.

I guess the bottom line is this: our clothes shouldn't punish us. Adam and Eve may have been acting out of guilt when they first put some on, but that was a long time ago. The debt's been paid.

—*I Think, Therefore I Have a Headache*

Celebrating Camaraderie

● ● ● Luci Swindoll

few years ago I was fortunate enough to have been invited as a speaker for a "conference afloat," a seminar cruise sponsored by my brother Chuck's radio ministry. The Insight for Living staff had chosen the theme "Experience the Fellowship" for the weeklong cruise. No other motto could have depicted the camaraderie any better!

For seven fun-filled days, the twelve hundred of us on board the ship spent every moment enjoying the entertainment, worship, fun, food, new friendships, and the breathtaking sights of the Caribbean islands. I can't imagine a better setting for celebrating camaraderie! We had at our disposal dozens of on-board shops, lounges, a movie theater, a huge library, a television studio, a game room, three swimming pools, a huge sun deck, and even an ice cream parlor. Sheer luxury. The islands provided plenty of white sandy beaches lined with umbrellas, swaying palm trees, wonderful calypso bands serenading us with island melodies, and beautiful turquoise water teeming with a kaleidoscope of fish and sea life. Insight for Living held daily Bible lessons on the life of Moses, offered early morning aerobic classes for those of us who had taken advantage of the ship's seven daily meals, sponsored activities for teenagers, singles, and adult groups, and gathered us all together for lots of music and song. All needs and desires were met for the body, soul, and spirit. But the best and most memorable part of the whole week was the camaraderie.

Every day I followed the Insight motto and experienced the fellowship. Among old friends, among new acquaintances, the theme of the cruise continually manifested itself. My favorite times were at Table 151, where I had been assigned for mealtimes. The eight of us became fast friends almost upon our first encounter. And together, we proved to be a notorious collection of funsters, punsters, pranksters, and gangsters in a mild but off-the-wall sense. Each mealtime was spiced with craziness, frivolity, harebrained chatter, wild "but true" stories, recounting of various escapades, spilling of embarrassing confessions, telling of jokes, spinning of fantasies, gales of laughter, plenty of high jinks and picture taking, and general nuttiness.

The last night of the cruise, in addition to the three already planned festivities, Table 151 decided to have its own farewell celebration. We had drawn names for gift-giving, and that evening we presented each other with zany limericks, songs, and ditties, along with such presents as a homemade collage of the cruise, poems, relics from the islands, and I even got a live hermit crab (which I mistook for a tarantula). We were the object of a few stares and raised eyebrows, but I cannot remember having so much fun. No doubt about it. Friends are *indeed* "the sunshine of life. . . ."

The morning we disembarked from our week of fun and frolic, picture, if you will, everyone from the Insight for Living Conference sitting around in one of the ship's larger lounges, awaiting an announcement over the loudspeaker that the ship had passed customs and its passengers could leave. The eight of us were sitting together one last time, continuing our marathon conversations and laughter, when suddenly, over the speaker system came this unexpected disclosure: "Will

Luci Swindoll of Cabin B188 please come to the purser's office and pay her bar bill?"

I could have died. Naturally, the whole place exploded into yells, jeers, finger pointing, and laughter. Here I was, one of Insight for Living's guest speakers for twelve hundred Christians, ignoring an outstanding bar bill. No matter the fact that it was for two Diet Pepsis I had signed for the first day of the cruise, which I had forgotten about—and that was *before* I changed cabins. I guess the "outstanding bar bill" is one thing I'll never live down.

We ended the cruise with hugs and tears and more laughter, promising to rendezvous again. My outrageous table companions and I had formed an unusually strong bond of friendship in seven short clays, a bond strengthened and enhanced by our kinship as children of God.

With comrades like that on your joyful journey, how can you help *but* celebrate?

. . . .

—*You Bring the Confetti, God Brings the Joy*

In Search of a Giggle

● ● ● Patsy Clairmont

My friend Carolyn gave me a magnet for my refrigerator that reads, "There's only one more shopping day until tomorrow."

That made me giggle aloud. I love giggle gifts because a dose of laughter is a gift in and of itself. The magnet business seems to be soaring these days, and I think it's because the makers have discovered the marketability of a good giggle-phrase.

One of my favorites is, "Mom, I'll always love you, but I'll never forgive you for washing my face with spit on your hankie." I howled at that one the first time I saw it because it's so true—we moms do that. My kids didn't see the humor, as they have been the direct recipients of that family-cleaning solvent.

I didn't laugh as hard when a friend sent me one that announced, "Be nice to me! With a minimum of effort, I can make things very difficult!" Ouch! Now, there's a gal who knows me too well.

Recently, I received a magnet that proclaimed, "If you think you're too small to be effective, you've never been in bed with a mosquito."

What day couldn't use a hearty chuckle? If I can laugh aloud, I don't even mind that my eyes narrow to slits, leaving me discombobulated.

Have you ever wanted to make your own magnets? I have. Here are the possibilities:

Menopause: a target for heat-seeking devices
Need a facelift? Try smiling!
Hormones: emotional chiggers
Trifocals: triple ripple

Well, you can sure tell my age. But since I can't change the modifications or the complications that come with maturing, let me toss back my head and chortle.

How long has it been since you laughed yourself sane?

Today, go in search of a giggle—you won't be sorry, no matter your age. And remember to give some giggles to others along the way.

— All Cracked Up

Angerless Charade

●●● Sheila Walsh

*W*hen I was fifteen years old, I played the part of Anger inside the mind of a man who was about to commit murder. It was a very avant-garde play, each character an emotion. My mother thought that *Little Women* would have been a better choice, but our hip new English teacher had moved beyond the classics.

I have no idea why she chose me to play Anger as I was a very mild-mannered teenager. She must have thought each one of us had a cauldron bubbling just below the surface. But as I learned my lines, I struggled to find my cauldron! By dress rehearsal our teacher was on the edge.

"Is that supposed to be anger? You're not mad enough to spank a hamster!"

"I'm trying," I said.

"Well, try harder—where is your anger? Tap into the rage!"

"I don't have any—I'm a Baptist!"

. . . .

—I'm Not Wonder Woman, But God Made Me Wonderful!

Living in God's House

••• Luci Swindoll

> Practice hospitality.
> —Romans 12:13

When I was little I had a set of Tinker Toys that I loved. Even now, I still love Tinker Toys. I've made bridges, houses, wagons, forts, cages, and furniture out of Tinker Toys.

And I love Lincoln Logs. By overlapping enough grooved ends, you can create the Roman Coliseum, albeit a kind of rustic version. But with enough imagination it has a resemblance. Sort of. And I love LEGOS. I've made everything from robots to rocket launchers with LEGOS. To this day, somebody gives me a little set of LEGOS every year for Christmas. I've missed my calling; I was meant to be a child. I love to make things.

That's why I jumped at the idea of building my own house. *It'll be made out of giant Lincoln Logs*, I thought. Not only that, there was something exciting about leaving California after thirty years and heading back to Texas, my childhood state. For the past six years, my friends here had welcomed me with open arms to stay in their guest room during the summer and fall (our busiest travel seasons at Women of Faith). Finally, in 2004, it made sense for me to actually relocate here; so now it was my opportunity to roll out a welcome mat.

After talking with a builder and choosing a lot in Frisco, north of Dallas and not far from the WOF office, the plans were put into place. The next thing I did was buy a "house book"—a big fat binder to keep all my drawings, doodlings, notes, and lists in one place. This undertaking was going to be, without doubt, one of the most interesting adventures I'd ever known—challenging, maddening, thrilling, exhilarating, and stupefying . . . sometimes on the same day or within the same hour, but I was up for it. After all, I was only seventy-two, and it sounded like child's play to actually *build* a dream house.

When I made the decision to leave California and head for Texas, I was inundated with offers from friends and even strangers to help: Can I bring lunch? Can I help you pack? Can I drive with you to Texas? Can I feed your dog? Well, I didn't have a dog, but had I, somebody would have offered to feed him.

When I got here, Texas was just as gracious in her welcome as California had been in her farewell. My Texas buddies and I watched my house go up in fits and spurts. We prayed over the foundation, walls, roof, and yard. We pooled our resources of time and money as some folks planned on-site picnics while others brought Starbucks and brownies.

The day it was time for my furniture to leave its storage place and waltz in the door, I had so many helpers they almost had to wear nametags. I even had matching black T-shirts made with a white logo reading, "Team Luci." My friends proved that now-famous Home Depot motto: "You can do it. We can help." They epitomized the Golden Rule of Scripture: "Do to others as you would have them do to you" (Luke 6:31). When everybody pitches in, the world seems like a better place and the work is a lot more fun, don't you think? Teamwork! A God-given concept.

I actually moved in on Labor Day. I signed all the papers thirty days before, but because of the warmth and love of the friends with whom I was staying, they encouraged me to take my time to settle in. "Keep the new house as your 'project,' Luci, but don't move in until you're ready." So I did exactly that. I loved that lingering spirit of acceptance and camaraderie.

Now that I'm *in here*, I'm having a great time. I have a 480-square-foot library with my collection of treasured books and paintings. I've unpacked boxes whose contents I hadn't seen in decades—love letters between my parents; my brothers' and my report cards from grammar, junior high, and high school; oil paintings by my mother and aunt; scrapbooks of my grand-mothers'; old fishing gear of my dad's and granddad's. The list goes on. What fun to dig around in all that stuff.

I'm actually not settled yet, because I keep thinking of things to hang or move or alphabetize. Not long ago I put my old record collection in order. In every box, bag, corner, nook, and cranny there's something else to unwrap, unpack, undo, or unwind that's been tucked away for eons. It's a treasure trove from the past, the museum of my life. (Or maybe a packrat's hideout.)

My greatest joy is throwing parties, having meetings, doing photo shoots, and enjoying out-of-town friends in the guest room. Marilyn Meberg gave me a plaque to hang at the front door that reads, "The ornament of a house is the friends who frequent it" (Ralph Waldo Emerson), and my house is always full of ornaments. And here's why: immediately after the foundation was poured, I came here (in the rain) with a few close friends and a screwdriver. Into the wet cement I carved an inscription that's become my precept: *This house is dedicated to God. 04/07/04. L. Swindoll.* Wringing wet that rainy night, all of us put our hands in the air and sang "To God Be the Glory." I don't know that I've ever been more excited or overwhelmed. I was building my first home, had just given it to God, planned to live here soon, and had committed myself to mortgage pay-ments until I was 101. *Life doesn't get any better than that!*

Everything I do in this house is governed by that phrase, and I've said it to myself dozens of times since then: *This is God's house.* It first started when a group of us had a birthday bash here for my brother Chuck: *God's house!* And it continued when the Women of Faith executive staff held a meeting around my dining table: *God's house!* There have been six or eight video and photo shoots here where the library had to be completely rearranged and wires and microphones put in precarious places, but so what? It's *God's house.* When things go "bump" in the night or a strange noise occurs in my backyard, I go back to sleep with the assurance that I'm in good hands because this is *God's house.* I never forget it. The joy of that phrase welcomes me home and helps me reach out to others. Dedicating my home to Him may be the best thing I ever did in my life. The onus of responsibility is off me, and the decisions for reaching out to others are already made. (Every now and then when I see a dust ball here or there, I do wonder why God never cleans His own house!)

I'm to the place where I keep the porch light on, the welcome mat out, and the Pizza Hut phone number in my billfold. You have no idea how far I've come from being a contented loner to this neighborhood. I used to spend hours reading adventure books like *The Worst Journey in the World,* and now I'm designing new ideas for place cards for one of the best dinner parties on the planet. God not only enlarged my surroundings, but He enlarged my heart. It's a great feeling.

And I thought Tinker Toys, Lincoln Logs, and LEGOS were fun! This is much better. God has given me a dwelling place that carries with it a joy I've never known before, and it's His joy that flows over the edges and onto my guests.

. . . .

— *Contagious Joy*

Weighty Matters

●●● Patsy Clairmont

Now I've heard it all! I know that we, the public, have proven ourselves vulnerable to scams, and I realize that the world is on a perpetual diet, but now we can laugh our weight off? I mean, what happened to the theory that round people are jovial? Did we pack that idea away with hula hoops and mood rings? Wouldn't all of us giddy, girthy girlfriends be the first to notice if we could chuckle till our buckle cinched?

According to some joyologists (uh-huh, *joyologists*—those given to the promotion of joy), you can lose weight if you guffaw daily. So, does this mean we can titter till our tummies tuck? Or better yet, chortle till the cellulite runs smooth? I'm afraid I'd have to be permanently hysterical to accomplish that task.

Can't you see it now? A world emphasis on belly laughing, with people lining up single file around the block, waiting to slip into a joy booth so they can laugh off lunch. Or employers offering health incentives for workers who snicker heartily. Or etched joy lines on our countenance being applauded because they indicate our amiableness rather than our need for Botox.

We live in a "make me happy" and "make life easy" society. Our humor wanes when we are made to wait or wonder. And for heaven's sake, don't make us wonder. We have to know, and we have to know in a microwave moment.

But suppose you're not like I am. (How presumptuous of me to think you are!) Perhaps you love wondering and you are a superb waiter . . . Yeah, sure. Think about it. When was the last time you strummed your fingers on the counter because the microwave was too slow, the traffic light didn't turn quickly enough, the express lane doddered, your pastor preached too long, or your dog couldn't decide which blade of grass to water?

Waiting weighs. And wondering—well, it's downright pudgy with pressure. I want to know where all the boats and airplanes disappeared to in the Bermuda Triangle. Don't you? What really happened to Amelia Earhart? I know her plane went down, but where? And why are my thighs sticking out farther than my hips?

These things mystify me. I like the tidiness of a package with all the ribbons tied up in a bow. I despise "To be continued" in a series. I don't want to be left sitting on the edge of my chair. I like resolution. Not knowing doesn't tickle me; not a solitary giggle will come forth from my anatomy when I'm left to stew.

Have you ever wondered why God designed us with the ability to laugh and to cry? I guess He knew we would need to do both as a way to pour off emotional excess; otherwise, we might blow a gasket. And gasket blowing is so untidy.

I've heard it said that hearty laughter sends fresh shipments of oxygen to the brain, which causes it to loosen up. Hmm, if it can loosen up my brain, then maybe, just maybe, the joyologists are right, and it could loosen up my jeans. That would be great. Then I wouldn't have to unsnap them to eat, sit, travel, and breathe.

I'd much rather chuckle myself fit than deny myself indulgences, but I have this nagging feeling I may need to do both.

. . . .

—All Cracked Up

We Are Relaxed

● ● ● Marilyn Meberg

One of the richest sources of humor lies within ourselves and our own experiences. Many times, however, we fail to acknowledge or even recognize that source of humor. When we take ourselves and our lives too seriously, we miss opportunities for a good laugh, and the tension this produces can kill future laughs before they are even born. A good laugh can make us relax or "mellow out." Let me cite one of my unnecessarily uptight responses to motherhood when my son, Jeff, was eighteen months old.

Jeff was hopelessly addicted to his pacifier. This concerned me because he looked mildly moronic with that rubber plug perpetually hanging out of his mouth, and he smelled bad as well. The rubber literally began to rot from constant use, and the smell of its decay clung to Jeff wherever he went.

The obvious solution of providing a new pacifier didn't work because he flatly refused any contact with one. I thought, *Why on earth would anyone in their right mind refuse a brand-new, inoffensive pacifier when it provides a classier look and a better aroma?*

Clearly this child was not concerned with aesthetics.

As the days dragged on, the odor intensified. I became desperate; my desperation produced tension. I studied Jeff as he would "plug in" his rank, little aid-to-peace, turning it slightly in his mouth until he achieved exactly the right feel. Then it hit me. He was attached to the old pacifier because it had ridges that conformed exactly to the contours of his mouth. It was a custom fit! It was familiar—homey—comfortable. The new one was foreign—sterile—stiff. At that moment I determined to form ridges on the new pacifier. There was only one way to do this—I would simply have to break it in myself!

I was well aware of the absurdity of this plan. The picture of a mother so driven by desperation that she would actually do what I was planning to do did amuse me. Nevertheless, in spite of the glimpse of humor I saw, I remained inordinately serious. I even entertained the possibility of Jeff and I developing a deeper level of camaraderie and identification as we went about each day sucking our mutual pacifiers.

On the first morning of this plan's enactment, Jeff settled in to watch *Captain Kangaroo*. As he plugged in, I sat down beside him and also plugged in. It took awhile for him to notice me, but when he did, he was vehement in his response. With a determined "No!" he yanked the pacifier out of my mouth and threw it on the floor. This happened several times; each time I tried to explain that Jeff had his pacifier and Mommy had hers, and we were going to enjoy them together. (Incidentally, there is nothing enjoyable or even pacifying about sucking a pacifier. The little rubber center threatened to activate the gag impulse in me, my mouth became dry, and my lips tired from pooching out!) Jeff was unmoved by my explanation. Throughout the day, whenever Jeff saw it in my mouth, he would dash up to me, wrench it from my lips, and throw it on the floor. He skulked about the house in an attempt to catch me "at it." Since my plan distressed Jeff, I determined to take to the pacifier when he was safely put away.

That evening, shortly after Jeff had gone to bed, my husband Ken and I were sitting on the couch reading the paper.

He made an interesting comment and I lowered my paper in response. He exhibited the same shock and revulsion to my pacifier-stuffed mouth as Jeff had earlier. Later that night, when I thought Ken was asleep, I reached over to the night-stand and noiselessly slipped the pacifier in my mouth. After a few minutes Ken raised up on an elbow and demanded, "What's that munching sound?" I had no idea I was audibly munching. I was then informed that no man in his right mind would go to bed with a woman who slept with a pacifier.

The number of hours available to me for ridge-development were lessening all the time, but a workable pattern subsequently developed. I simply plugged in during Jeff's morning and afternoon naps, which gave me at least two hours a day to work on my project.

One morning about ten days later, I was vacuuming the living room, pacifier firmly in place. I thought I heard a knock. Without turning off the vacuum, I opened the door a few inches and peeked around it. To my chagrin, there stood a salesman with a satchel full of brushes. As his face registered a look of complete bewilderment, I quickly unplugged both vacuum and pacifier. He had not said a word; he just stared. Seeing him back away, I felt compelled to explain what I was doing.

"Now wait a minute," I said. "I know this looks peculiar but, you see, this pacifier isn't mine! Well, what I mean is . . . it's my little boy's . . . he's asleep right now . . . I only suck on it when he's asleep. It upsets him if I suck on it when he's awake. It upsets my husband, too, for that matter! The only reason I've got this one in my mouth is because the other one got to smelling so bad I couldn't stand it any longer."

He continued staring at me. Just as I was about to launch into the importance of forming ridges and to show him that I was actually about to accomplish my goal, he burst into a fit of raucous laughter. He laughed, gasped, choked, and then laughed some more. I thought, *Well, really! I didn't invite this perfect stranger to my door . . . and now, having caught me at a rather awkward moment, he has the audacity to gasp and wheeze in the face of my explanations!* When he managed to get his breath, he raised one hand weakly in an almost defensive gesture and said, "Lady, I don't know what you are doing, and I don't care. I just want you to know you've made my day." He then went into another fit of laughter and lurched down the sidewalk toward his parked car. Strangely enough, I haven't seen him again, but it's just as well since I prefer to buy my brushes at the supermarket.

Several days later, without the slightest hesitation, Jeff took the pacifier I had broken in; he never knew what I had done. (I confessed ten years later. Happily, by then he had kicked his habit.)

—*Choosing the Amusing*

©2004 Bunny Hoest. Used by permission.

"You know, Mom, for a minute there—when you said, 'For the last time, no!'—I almost thought you meant it."

Part 2

Laugh? I Thought I'd Die!

Laughing When It Hurts

• • • • •

Today is the tomorrow you worried about yesterday— but not nearly enough.

Putting on the Ritz

● ● ● Cathy Lee Phillips

he Ritz-Carlton? Well, maybe I can adjustment my schedule," Jennifer said breathlessly.

The rat! For several weeks I had begged Jennifer to go to the beach with me but scheduling conflicts kept her close to home. I needed the beach—the majesty, the constant rolling of the waves, the countless grains of sand on the beach. I was thirty-five years old and reeling from my husband's recent death. I was angry and seeking God plus a little pampering. Suddenly the Ritz-Carlton not only sounded possible, it sounded downright necessary. Being a savvy, independent woman, I would go to the beach by myself!

The Ritz-Carlton, Amelia Island, Florida was offering a special rate of $159 per night for a suite that normally rented for $650 per night. I had never visited a Ritz but I knew their reputation for being the ultimate in indulgence and luxury.

"Book it!" I told my travel agent.

I tried to fight the urge, but I ultimately called Jennifer to gloat. After all, what good is going to the Ritz-Carlton if you can't gloat about it? Because our husbands had pastored neighboring United Methodist Churches, we saw each other often and our friendship had quickly grown.

Jennifer was a teacher, having a long summer vacation, so it seemed sensible that she could accompany me to the beach.

It seemed that she had no time for pitiful little me—until I mentioned the Ritz-Carlton.

Three days later we turned toward Florida, jabbering constantly as we traveled. As we neared the island, however, we began to think seriously about something near and dear to both of us—snacks! We had no idea what edibles the hotel would offer so we made a quick stop at a convenience store for the basics:

- two cases of caffeine-free Diet Coke
- Double Stuf Oreos
- cheese and crackers
- cherry Pop Tarts (for breakfast)
- one bag of Almond Joy candy bars
- a massive bag of bright-orange cheese puffs (We could survive for weeks from the thousands of cheese puffs that cost only ninety-nine cents.)
- one disposable razor (Jennifer had forgotten to shave her legs.)

We both struggled to stuff this enormous bag of cheese puffs into the plastic shopping bag from the service station. We moved carefully to avoid a cheese puff blast.

Twenty minutes later we drove onto Amelia Island, still jabbering so much that we missed the turn to the hotel. In the distance, though, we spotted a large hotel with a Mediterranean look complete with a beautiful aqua roof.

"Look at that place," I commented. "It is beautiful and has to be beachfront. We'll drive toward it. Surely the Ritz-Carlton will be nearby."

Wistfully, Jennifer said, "I'd like to stay at a place like that just once before I die."

"Forget it, girlfriend. We are preacher's wives and the real people of the world. It will never happen!"

"Maybe if we saved our dollars until we are ninety we could afford at least one night."

"It will never happen," the realist in me said.

But as we followed the signs and made the last turn, we faced that very building and read a sign that boasted, "Welcome to the Ritz-Carlton."

I stopped the car.

"I feel completely outclassed," I whispered as I looked at my old shorts and tank top. And Jennifer still had not shaved her legs.

"We can't go up there," Jennifer whined.

But logic took over. It was after 6:00 p.m. and my credit card was on file. I had already paid for the night. I was going in!

An army of uniformed attendants descended upon the car. "Welcome to the Ritz-Carlton. May we get your bags? Please let me valet park your car while you check in. Did you have a pleasant trip?"

Our old clothes were hideous and people were staring at Jennifer's hairy legs. I wanted to get through the lobby quickly and without incident. Because the reservation was in my name, I was in charge of check-in, leaving Jennifer in charge of luggage. I was completing the paperwork when I suddenly heard something akin to a mild nuclear explosion behind me. Instinctively, I turned around and, to my horror, observed orange cheese puffs covering the marbled floor of the Ritz-Carlton. Meanwhile, Jennifer looked like a granny picking butterbeans. Pulling out the front of her old tank top, she grabbed wayward cheese puffs from the floor and furniture. The bellman begged her to stop, but she kept going until she had about three pounds of cheese puffs wrapped in the ugliest tank top on Amelia Island.

I wanted to register under an alias!

The bellman finally led Jennifer to our accommodations on the sixth floor. I followed them . . . from a distance! The bellman waited until I caught up before opening the door to our opulent suite. The sitting room was decorated beautifully in tones of green with an overstuffed sofa and chairs and a large color television. A separate bedroom was equally posh with two queen beds, desks, and a tall armoire holding another large television. An immense hallway held two large closets complete with thick terry-cloth Ritz-Carlton robes. A large private balcony overlooked the beach and a perfectly manicured courtyard. Three separate marble bathrooms completed the ensemble.

"Are your accommodations suitable, Mrs. Phillips?" the bellman asked.

"I suppose," I replied, trying to sound like I did this every day.

When he left the room, Jennifer and I squealed with delight. The place was gorgeous and it was ours for the next three days!

"Where is the phone?" Jennifer shrieked. "I have to call Dick and tell him about this place!"

We looked around the suite and found a variety of phones, six in all. Choosing one next to the sofa, Jennifer remarked, "Wow, look at all these buttons! I wonder what they all do."

"Just don't call Alaska or do anything to embarrass me," I instructed, remembering that the registration was in my name only.

Lifting the receiver, Jennifer called her husband. Dick was not home but, in our excitement, we proceeded to leave a very long, very silly, ridiculous message describing our arrival at the Ritz-Carlton. With great animation we related everything—the young men who met our car, the bellman, and the beautiful lobby layered with three inches of cheese puffs.

Jennifer described the room in detail—from the posh furnish-
ings to the magnificent view.

While she talked, I explored the suite and found, to my
amazement, that each bathroom was equipped with a telephone. It hung on the wall next to the toilet. So, as Jennifer
continued to babble, I picked up the extension from the bathroom in the foyer and said, "Hey, Dick, I am using the phone
in the first bathroom in the suite. Three bathrooms for two
people—is this a great country or what? Just think, I can go
to the bathroom and talk to you at the same time. Just in case
you don't believe me, I'll prove it!"

I held the receiver at an angle that would pick up the
sound of the toilet as I flushed it. On a roll, I walked into the
next bathroom.

"Hello, Dick. I am in bathroom number two. It has a gray
marbled floor, a large tub, and a mirror that covers the whole
wall. And guess what? There is a phone next to this toilet,
too! Just listen."

And I flushed toilet number two.

"Dick, this is me in bathroom number three. We have
another marble floor and a shower with a glass door. There
are tons of towels and Ritz-Carlton toiletries. And, of course,
there is a phone. Now hear this!"

And I flushed toilet number three.

Jennifer and I were red-faced with laughter by the time we
completed our bizarre message. We were having a great time!

"Now, I've just got to call Mom," Jennifer laughed.

"Wait! Let me get to the bathroom." I crossed the room to
start flushing again while Jennifer punched buttons on the
phone. When she picked up the receiver, she made an odd
sound, turned pale, and placed the receiver on the base.

"What?" I demanded. "What's wrong?"

For a few brief seconds she was completely quiet and still pale. Then she spoke in a subdued voice.

"Someone from the hotel office spoke to me when I began dialing," she relayed. "I could hear giggling in the background and they gave me some phone instructions."

"What instructions?" I practically shouted.

Obviously horrified, Jennifer said, "They said, 'Mrs. Phillips, before placing your next call you may wish to depress the conference call button.'"

My stomach churned. This meant only one thing—the staff in the hotel office had heard our entire ridiculous, absurd, laughable conversation, crowned with three toilet flushes! I turned pale myself and dropped on the sofa next to my former friend.

For me, the most awful part of this nightmare was that the operator had called her Mrs. Phillips. The Ritz-Carlton did not know Jennifer at all; they only knew the room was registered to Mrs. Phillips. They had my credit card. They knew my home address.

"I'm never leaving this room," I said, completely humiliated.

Jennifer confessed, "I think I want to go home."

Silence filled the room—at least for a few minutes until Jennifer began a soft giggle that quickly matured into a loud belly laugh. It took me a few minutes longer for me to see the humor in the situation because I was, after all, Mrs. Phillips, the registered guest.

We laughed until our sides hurt. We laughed until we rolled off the sofa and onto the dark green carpet. We laughed until tears rolled down our faces. We laughed until we each had to use one of the three bathrooms in the suite.

"These people will think we are just two naïve preacher's wives from the country," Jennifer pouted.

"We are," I said, and the laughter began all over again.

Happily, we did not go home, nor did we hide in our room for the rest of our trip. We took full advantage of the hotel's amenities—the swimming pools, the hot tubs, the beautiful beach and gardens. We enjoyed high tea in a cozy setting overlooking the ocean. We even found the courage to use the telephone again. Our three days passed so quickly that leaving was difficult and we promised ourselves we would return one day.

Luckily, I have returned many times since that first trip to the Ritz-Carlton. In fact, it is my favorite get-away! At no time, though, has the hotel refused my reservation because of the behavior Jennifer and I exhibited on our first visit. On the contrary, each trip to the Ritz-Carlton is wonderful and I return home rested in body and spirit.

No trip quite compares to the first, of course. After months of grief and depression, I experienced real laughter again—not a wimpy little chuckle, but a body-aching, bladder clenching, tear-producing belly laugh.

It felt wonderful!

Is This a Disaster—or a Pimple-Level Problem?

● ● ● Max Lucado

*I*f God is our guardian, why do bad things happen to us?

Have they? Have bad things *really* happened to you? You and God may have different definitions for the word *bad*. Parents and children do. Look up the word *bad* in a middle-schooler's dictionary, and you'll read definitions such as "pimple on nose," "Friday night all alone," or "pop quiz in geometry." "Dad, this is really bad!" the youngster says. Dad, having been around the block a time or two, thinks differently. Pimples pass. And it won't be long before you'll treasure a quiet evening at home. Inconvenience? Yes. Misfortune? Sure. But *bad*? Save that adjective for emergency rooms and cemeteries.

What's bad to a child isn't always bad to a dad.

What you and I might rate as an absolute disaster, God may rate as a pimple-level problem that will pass. He views your life the way you view a movie after you've read the book. When something bad happens, you feel the air sucked out of the theater. Everyone else gasps at the crisis on the screen. Not you. Why? You've read the book. You know how the good guy gets out of the tight spot. God views your life with the same confidence. He's not only read your story . . . He wrote it. His perspective is different, and His purpose is clear.

God uses struggles to toughen our spiritual skin.

Consider it a sheer gift, friends, when tests and challenges come at you from all sides. You know that under pressure, your faith-life is forced into the open and shows its true colors. So don't try to get out of anything prematurely. Let it do its work so you become mature and well-developed, not deficient in any way. (James 1:2–4 MSG)

. . . .

—Come Thirsty

Cheer Up!

● ● ● Barbara Johnson

When things go bad, cheer up. Remember, they could always be worse. And, of course, if they do get worse, it will make your heart smile to remember that when it's this bad, it has to get better soon.

. . . .

—Daily Splashes of Joy

Surviving All Those Aggravating A-teds

● ● ● Thelma Wells

Count it all joy when you fall into various trials, knowing
that the testing of your faith produces patience.
—James 1:2–3

During those stressful days as our daughter Vikki neared the end of her difficult pregnancy, my cell phone went on the blink. Isn't that just like one of those whiz-bang space-age gadgets to die when you should be depending on it most urgently? With all that was going on, I *had* to have a working cell phone. I couldn't bear the thought that Vikki might need me and be unable to reach me.

Someone took it back to the phone store for me to get it checked out, but it couldn't be repaired. So this kind person bought me a new phone—but didn't get it activated because I had pictures stored on the old phone that I wanted to keep, and in order to keep them they had to be downloaded to a computer and then reloaded onto the new phone. No one had time to do that downloading and reloading; we were all overloaded with too many other loads!

Finally, the next day, I attempted the task, but nothing would work. The pictures wouldn't copy. We even took the phone back to the store and asked the technician to try it, but he had no success either. After two frustrating days, I made an executive decision: I threw away the old phone, photos and all, so I could get the new phone activated. Whew! What a relief it was to just move on and put an end to the lost time, lost pictures, lost calls, maybe lost business. (And possibly a few lost friends. Believe it or not, I tend to get cranky when a technical gadget refuses to cooperate, and since the gadget doesn't care what kind of mood I'm in, I sometimes "download" my feelings on whoever happens to be standing nearby.)

I had a new cell phone that worked. But the relief didn't last long.

The next day, a Thursday, I flew to Detroit for a Women of Faith conference, and as I walked out of the house, I picked up my husband's cell phone charger instead of mine. I spent so much time talking on the phone in the airports and during the cab ride in Detroit that the phone was dead by the time I got to the hotel. As soon as I realized I'd brought the wrong charger, my wonderful assistant, Pat, who never breaks or loses or picks up the wrong anything, called home and arranged for the right charger to be shipped to me overnight. Finally, Friday afternoon, I could charge up my cell phone and keep in touch with Vikki and my grandchild-to-be back in Texas. Everything was rosy.

Until Saturday.

Would you believe, when I headed out to the arena Saturday morning, I walked right out of the hotel room and left that cell phone behind!? So, after all I'd been through to make sure I stayed in touch with my family while I was away, I went through the entire conference on Saturday without a phone and without a clue about how Vikki was doing. And, I might add, without a shred of patience with myself for being so addle-brained.

By any chance are you smiling? Have you ever had one of those weeks when things start out wrong and just keep on going, and you get increasingly frustrated, aggravated, agitated, irritated, and all those other "*a*-teds"?

Now let me ask you this: Did it make a good story? Did you share it with your family and friends and make them smile? (It's always easier to laugh at someone else's "*a*-teds" rather than your own, isn't it?) Isn't it a relief to finally get through some ongoing trial and be able to look back on it and laugh?

I'm just guessing, but the apostle James was probably talking about a more serious trial than an uncooperative cell phone (and a forgetful mind) when he wrote that we're to "count it all joy." But I can tell you for sure that a joyful attitude sure makes trials easier to bear, no matter how trivial or terrible the trial is. Added to the Romans 8:28 promise that the Lord makes "all things work together for good to those who love God" (NKJV), it's easy to see that our Creator expects us to cling to our faith and keep a positive mind-set, no matter what kinds of problems we're facing

. . . .

—*Listen Up, Honey*

Sharing Comfort in the Cesspool

● ● ● Barbara Johnson

Those who hope in the LORD will renew their strength.
They will soar on wings like eagles; they will run and
not grow weary, they will walk and not be faint.
—Isaiah 40:31

*W*hen people around us are rejoicing and praising God while we are struggling through deep mire and floodwaters, we begin to wonder if something is wrong with us. We begin to feel like second-class Christians. And then the final straw comes if these people who are being blessed and who don't face the problems we do are quick to give us the glib answers: "Just praise the Lord . . . You are just not praising the Lord enough . . . What you need to do is take your stand . . . Just praise the Lord!"

When the floodwaters of the cesspool have come up to your very soul, you don't need challenges; you need COMFORT. You need a friend to come alongside and say, "I am hurting with you . . . I am standing with you . . . I am weeping with you. I am undergirding you as best I can. Link your shield of faith with mine and somehow we will make it together."

Please spare me the ghastly details of your happiness!

. . . .

—*Daily Splashes of Joy*

The Fun of Imperfection

● ● ● Sandi Patty

I've heard it said that we learn more from our mistakes than from our successes. If that's true, I should be a genius by now! I think there's a corollary to that adage for blended families coping with being bigger than they were before: bigger families have bigger problems and make bigger messes, so we have bigger things to laugh about later (assuming we survive the big messes we make). In fact, sometimes it's the things that go wrong that end up meaning the most to us.

Case in point: our family vacation in Greece. Actually it was part of a cruise event I hosted annually for a group called Forever Friends. Usually we sailed the Caribbean, but that year I wanted to do something special, so I set up the Forever Friends cruise in the Mediterranean and brought along Don and the kids as my "special talent." (Hey, whatever it takes.)

So, after months and months of planning, we finalized a complicated but thrilling itinerary for the ten of us in conjunction with the cruise. We would fly from Indianapolis to Atlanta, then on to London, where we would change airlines and fly to Italy to enjoy a couple of days in Venice before joining our Forever Friends on the cruise ship. We would sail across the Mediterranean to Greece, and then our family would spend some additional days sightseeing and soaking up the wonders of the ancient world.

Ask my kids today about that elaborate trip, and not one of them will mention visiting the Acropolis or the Parthenon. They don't remember a thing about Venice or cruising the Mediterranean either. What they like to talk about is, first, how we got stuck in the Atlanta airport for *two days*. We landed there just as a huge storm swept up the East Coast, closing the airport. The storm finally ended, but all the flights to London were full for the next two days. Well, maybe not full, but they didn't have ten empty seats, which is what we needed. So there we sat (and slept) on the floor of the airport for forty-eight hours.

The kids loved it. We played endless card games, we ate every kind of airport junk food available, we exercised by parading up and down the long concourse, and best of all, we talked and talked and talked.

Then came the next adventure: changing planes in London. Our connection was a little tight, and when we stopped at the desk and asked, the gate agent said pleasantly, "Your flight will be leaving from gate ninety." I don't remember what gate we'd come in at, but we all remember that it was a *long* way to gate ninety. We loaded up the mountain of luggage onto several baggage carts, put the smallest kids in the seats, and set off at a trot for the other end of the airport. But when we got there . . . it wasn't our flight! We realize *now* that the pleasant gate agent was saying, in her crisp British accent, "Your flight will be leaving from gate NINE-teen."

Now we were really late, so we made a quick U-turn and raced back up the concourse. Can you picture this galloping, ten-member assemblage of parents, kids, luggage, and carts frantically speeding through the airport? Can you do it without laughing? Not us!

But that wasn't the last adventure (and you'll notice there's still nothing about the Parthenon). We landed in

Venice and rushed off to the cruise ship (forget sightseeing; we had used up our two buffer days in Atlanta), arriving less than two hours before it departed. Then we sailed on over to Greece to do the sightseeing thing.

One afternoon in between tours, we found ourselves with a little free time, and we rounded up the kids, waved down two taxis, and asked the lead driver to take us to a family beach. The taxis dropped us off, Don paid the fare, then we made the short walk down to the beach. And yes, indeed, it was a family beach, full of parents and youngsters, teenagers, middle-aged sunbathers, and old people, all frolicking in the surf, jogging over the sand, even playing badminton and volleyball—*most of them topless if not totally nude!*

We hurried our little covey of big-eyed children down to the water, urging them to watch where they stepped (hoping they would keep their eyes on their feet instead of the naked people around us). Some of the kids handled the situation better than others, but Jonathan, in particular, was mortified by where we'd taken him. "Mom, we can't stay here!" he said.

"Honey, let's just make the best of it. Go on with the others and play in the water a little while; just ignore those other people. You're from Indiana! Go enjoy the ocean! Have fun and don't think about anything else," I told him.

Reluctantly, Jon headed down to the water to join Don and the rest of the family. He splashed around in the surf for a while, but then a big wave rolled in unexpectedly and smacked him right in the face. He turned and ran headlong up the beach, his eyes full of salt water, and tumbled right into a topless, middle-aged, female jogger, his face landing right in her chest. Poor Jonathan was so mortified, when he finally got back to our pile of stuff, he curled up in a little ball, covered his head completely with a beach towel, and refused to open his eyes until we left. The rest of the kids came up later and said, "What's wrong with Jonathan?"

"Don't ask," I told them.

That trip full of missed planes and misadventures is just one instance of how we have come to appreciate (later) the things that go wrong even more than we do the things that go right.

. . . .

—*Life in the Blender*

If You're Happy and You Know It . . .

● ● ● Thelma Wells

*D*o you remember that old traditional song that says, "If you're happy and you know it, then your life will surely show it"? That should be a theme song for Christians everywhere! We can be joyful in a broken world, and we know it—because we know Jesus. And we know where we're goin' when this life is over. Sure, we'll have dark days and temporary setbacks, but the Bible tells us "our light and momentary troubles are achieving for us an eternal glory that far outweighs them all" (2 Corinthians 4:17). Now that's something to praise God about!

. . . .

—Listen Up, Honey

Lord, Did You Misunderstand?

● ● ● Natalie Grant

Ames, Iowa
Winter 2003

My curtain call was quickly approaching. I was on tour with several different bands, and as the only female, I had a dressing room completely to myself. I wanted to look my best that night, so I had spent a little extra time getting ready, pulling on the cutest pair of jeans, tall stiletto boots, and a sassy little black leather hat. Right before I headed out the door, I prayed the prayer I always pray before facing the stage lights: "Lord, be glorified through my music, and may the words of my mouth and the meditation of my heart please You."

My band members took their respective places, then I waltzed into the spotlight, smiling my brightest smile and eager to get started. It was going to be a good night. I could feel it.

As we started the first song, I could hear the enthusiastic roar of the five thousand people in the audience. Each face seemed to be filled with warm encouragement, and the crowd's expectant energy filled the auditorium. The groove my band was laying down felt great, and I was belting out "Keep on Shining" at the top of my lungs.

Then I fell off the stage.

Yes, you read that correctly. *I fell off the stage!* I don't know exactly what went wrong. I had done that set of music many times before and always managed to stay on my feet, but somehow, this time was different. I'd like to blame the incident on one of the floor monitors—a speaker that plays back the sound of the band and my voice so I can hear what's happening. But the truth is, those monitors were in the same spot on the stage they always were, and the one I tripped over certainly didn't jump out in front of me. But for some reason, on the last note of my first song, I walked right into it, lost my balance, flipped through an aerial movement that surely would have scored at least an 8 in any Olympic competition, and tumbled off the stage into the crowd.

At least part of me landed in the crowd; the other part was still dangling from the stage.

Fortunately (at least for me—the folks I fell on might not have felt so fortunate), people were standing right up against the platform, and they caught me. Otherwise I would have fallen right on my head. If I had been thinking, I could have pretended to crowd-surf, although I've never been one for mosh pits. (Okay, I've moshed in my mind many times but have never been quite cool enough to act it out.)

I guess the production crew had never seen an artist take a dive off the stage before, because none of them seemed to have a clue what to do. Finally the lighting engineer turned off the stage lights, probably hoping to diminish the sight of me sprawled between the edge of the stage and my human safety net. Thoughtfully, those kind people pushed me back up on the stage, where I lay for a moment curled up in the fetal position, probably thinking, *Lord, is there any chance you misunderstood when I asked that you would be glorified through my performance tonight? Maybe You thought I said horrified?*

I had been using a corded microphone, and as I went down, the mike went hurling into the crowd. Still lying on the stage but now hunched up like an armadillo, I pulled on the cord, yanking it in like a fishing line caught on a rock. Then I just lay there on the stage another moment, lost in the darkness, ready to burst into both tears and laughter at the same time.

Girl, you've got two choices, I told myself: *get off the stage while it's still dark and never show your face in Ames, Iowa, again, or get up and keep going.*

I got up.

I had injured my ankle in the fall, but the real injury was to my pride. Although I was embarrassed, humiliated, insecure, and unsure of myself, I finished my show. Some of the other artists on the tour helped me up onto a stool. My injured ankle made it difficult to stand, so I took off my stiletto boots and finished the rest of my set in my socks. I was just thankful they were clean. Then I looked down and saw my pinkie toe peeking out of a small hole . . .

. . . .

—*The Real Me*

Keep Your Joy, No Matter What

● ● ● Thelma Wells

The joy of the LORD is your strength.
—Nehemiah 8:10

There's this guy in the Bible that I visit fairly often. He's one of the coolest dudes I've ever gotten acquainted with. He's cool because he seems always to be focused and right on target regardless of what he's confronted with. Every time I visit him I see another intriguing quality that I missed the last time I went to his house. He lives in a chapter named for him found in the territory of the Old Testament, next door to his comrade Ezra and his boss's stepmother, Queen Esther.

"God is consolation." That's the meaning of his name. How cool is that? Nehemiah lived up to that name because whatever was going on around him, he'd turn to God and God would always give him consolation. Maybe that's why most of the time he had a great attitude, a smile on his face, and a passion for excellence. After all, he had a great job in the service of King Artaxerxes I Longimanus of Persia. The career was macho and dangerous, but Nehemiah was up for it. He was the cupbearer to the king, and his job was to sip the best wine from the vineyards and taste the most well-prepared and delicious food in the kingdom before the king drank or ate. The danger was, if the wine or food was poisoned, Nehemiah would get sick or die, thus preserving the health and life of the king. Not a problem for Nehemiah. His absolute confidence in his God made him all that and a bag of chips.

One day, however, Nehemiah got some disturbing news about his homeland and the conditions of the walls around Jerusalem. The walls of the holy city had been broken down, the gates were burned, and the people were in distress. This news troubled Nehemiah, and he wanted to fix everything for his countrymen. But as I said, he was cool. Instead of hurtling forward without being prepared, he mourned, fasted, prayed for direction from God, confessed and acknowledged the sins of his fellow Jews, reminded God of His promise to restore the Israelites, and asked God for success and favor with the king.

When he went into his boss's chambers one day, the king noticed that his cupbearer did not have the usual smile on his face and his attitude needed adjusting. This aroused the king's curiosity, and he asked Nehemiah what was wrong and what he wanted. Nehemiah was still cool. The brother did not answer the king until he whispered a prayer to God for wisdom. I'm sure Nehemiah's prayer was a fleeting thought or request. But when he did speak to the king, his words were from the heart of God.

The king responded with gracious favor and provided his cupbearer with rights of passage to go back to Judah, his motherland. Nehemiah's plan was to rebuild the walls and restore the city for the people. He had no architectural skills, no carpentry or masonry skills, but somehow he knew how to select the right team to work with him. At first he took three good men with him to check out the conditions of the walls and gates. But he didn't even let them in on what was really happening. He just told them, "The God of heaven will give us success" (Nehemiah 2:20). All during the rebuilding process,

Nehemiah prayed to God and listened for His instructions. God protected the people as they worked like Trojans by day and guarded the city by night.

You can imagine that anywhere there is a group of people, somebody's going to get on edge and start expressing their opinions or needs. There were poor people in Jerusalem who had good reason to complain. When Nehemiah discovered their complaints were merited, he did something about it. He rebuked the countrymen who were taking advantage of the poor and asked them to make a vow that they would knock it off and make restitution. All the guilty got back on track, renewed their reverence for God, and became obedient to the God of their fathers. Throughout all this Nehemiah stayed focused on his primary task of rebuilding the walls and restoring the people.

His enemies plotted to kill him and sent him false truths via messengers of doom. They were trying to wear him down. But Nehemiah always remembered from where his strength came, and he prayed, "Now strengthen my hands, Lord." God did! Finally, the enemy lost confidence. Nehemiah finished the walls and gates in fifty-two days. But his work of restoration was not over.

In a census count of the inhabitants of Jerusalem there were more than forty-two thousand men, not counting the women and children. Their ancestors had been in Babylonian captivity for seventy years, and this was a new generation of citizens who knew little about their original homeland. In the town center a solemn assembly was called by Nehemiah, who was now the governor. Ezra, the priest and scribe, and the Levite preachers read the Law of God to the people and interpreted it so those who had long been in exile could understand. When the people heard what the Book of Moses had to say and realized what their relatives had done to get them sent away from their rightful land into bondage, the people were grieved and began to cry and squall with bitter tears. But Mr. Cool knew how to recapture their joy. I can just hear Nehemiah now, talking loud, but in a loving, tender, authoritative voice: "Don't cry on such a day as this! For today is a sacred day before the Lord your God—it is time to celebrate with a hearty meal, and to send presents to those in need, for the joy of the Lord is your strength. You must not be dejected and sad!" (see Nehemiah 8:9–10).

We can learn some valuable lessons from this brother about how to live effectively in our present circumstances, no matter what they are. Throughout his adventure with the king of Persia, the people of Judah, and his enemies, Nehemiah remained focused on the assignments God had given him. When things got rough or decisions had to be made, he prayed. He took his cues from the only Source that is all-wise and can never misguide or make a mistake. He remained in such close communication with God that he was given divine insight in the moment. He knew when trouble was around and the enemy was trying to trick him.

One of the things that inspires me most when I visit Nehemiah is his joyful spirit. Throughout his adventure, he knew how to celebrate his accomplishments and see the good in what God was doing. The clincher was the big meeting in which folks tried to get all sensitive and emotional because of the past. They couldn't do nuttin' 'bout dat. They were home now. So Nehemiah put a stop to their whining before it got out of hand. He realized that if you feed folks and give them something to drink, add a little motivational speech, and get their minds on something larger than themselves, they can recapture their joy, even in the midst of sorrow.

Nehemiah kept his joy through all he experienced because he was constantly connected to the Joy Giver. Without God as your personal guide and consolation, there is no real joy in the adventure of life, only temporary happiness when things go your way. Your name may not mean "God of consolation," but you can enjoy the presence and direction of the One who is the Master Consoler, the One who can unleash wellsprings of joy in your heart and soul right where you are, right now.

— *The Great Adventure Devotional*

Filling Your Blessing Basket

● ● ● Sheila Walsh

Parents will tell their children what you have done.
They will retell your mighty acts, wonderful majesty,
and glory. And I will think about your miracles. They
will tell about the amazing things you do, and I will tell
how great you are. They will remember your great
goodness and will sing about your fairness.
—Psalm 145:4–7 NCV

I was born in Scotland, went to college in London, England, and first set foot on American soil during a summer mission trip when I was twenty years old. I remember looking out of the plane window as we circled Manhattan before landing at JFK airport in New York. Tears ran down my cheeks. It was so exciting to look at a skyline that I had seen in movies as a little girl and dreamt that perhaps one day I would get to visit.

By my late twenties, America had become home. I embraced almost everything that was new to me. I finally accepted that you are supposed to have that much ice in your soda, and they weren't trying to rip me off because I had a funny accent. In Scotland, anything more than two cubes of ice is viewed with great suspicion. I welcomed the concept of a bucket of popcorn with every movie. At home, if it's a long movie, you bring sandwiches!

The one thing I could not accept was pumpkin pie. After

my very first Thanksgiving meal in the hotel where I was staying, I visited the dessert table and picked up what I thought was treacle tart or my very favorite, sticky toffee pudding in pie form. When I put that first, most delectable forkful in my mouth, I nearly had a fit.

"What is this?" I whispered to an American friend who was eating with me.

"It's pumpkin pie," she said.

"Pumpkin as in 'look at all those pumpkins in the vegetable patch, Charlie Brown'?" I asked.

"Right, pumpkin pie; it's Thanksgiving!" she said.

"That is disgusting!" I replied. "Do they have any Brussels sprouts pie? Or how about some green bean pie?"

Despite my disgust with the "vegetable-in-sheep's-clothing" thing, Thanksgiving has become one of my favorite days of the year. I love that it's not sullied by receiving gifts, but rather it's a time to stop and thank God for every gift He has lavished on us every day. Life is so busy and demanding that I'm grateful for a reminder to just stop . . . stop and see everything with which our Father has surrounded us.

Giving thanks does wonders for me. It refocuses me on what's really important so that, instead of dwelling on the fact that our dog just dropped one of my new pale blue suede pumps down the toilet, I can celebrate the gift of her sweet face, loving nature, and commitment to follow me wherever I go.

Marcus Aurelius, a first-century Roman emperor, wrote that the most important thing a man can choose is how he thinks. We can dwell every day on the things that are not working and let them drag us down, or we can thank God for the simple gifts of grace He gives us every day, if we have a heart to see them.

When Barry's mom's liver cancer had spread to the degree that she was receiving in-home hospice care, she told me about the many people who dropped by every day to say hi or to bring some crab soup to try to tempt her to eat. "Sometimes you don't stop to think how many good friends you have until a time like this," Eleanor said. "I wish I had told them how much I appreciated them more often when I was well."

That thought sat on my shoulder like a small bird waiting to be fed. One March evening when we were visiting Eleanor in Charleston, Barry and I went out for a drive through the beautiful countryside. Suddenly the idea occurred to me: "Here's what I'd like to do," I said. "We'll have a good photo taken of you and Christian and me and get it enlarged, then cut it into pieces."

Barry looked at me as if the strain of his mom's illness had pushed me off a mental bridge. "Like a jigsaw puzzle," I explained. "We'll send a piece of the puzzle to each of our dear friends with a letter telling them why we're grateful to them, what they add to our lives, and how God has used them to fill in the missing pieces in our hearts. Then at Christmas we'll invite them to a party at our house. We'll ask them to bring their piece and give them a gift specially chosen to highlight what they mean to us."

Barry was still looking at me as if I needed more sleep. I pressed on as we women have to when they don't get it. "At the end of the evening we'll glue all the pieces back together, a visual picture of how our friends have added to our lives and how truly grateful we are for each one of them."

"What made you think of that?" Barry asked as we drove across the river.

"Don't you think it's a good idea?" I asked him.

"Sure I do," he replied, "but what made you think of it?"

"I don't really know. Sometimes I just want to find more ways to say thank you."

"So you just thought of that?" Barry pressed.

"Yes."

"And you're feeling all right?"

"Yes!"

I smiled. "It's like what we're trying to teach Christian. We tell him it's not enough just to say 'sorry' when he does something wrong. Instead we ask him to tell us what he's sorry for. So perhaps it's not always enough to say 'thanks' either. We need to say what we're grateful for."

As I lay in bed that night after swallowing the two aspirin Barry gave me, I thought about how the same principle applies to our relationship with God. Instead of just tossing off a "Hey, thanks!" now and then as we hustle through life, why not make it a practice to thank Him very specifically for His goodness to us and celebrate His love?

In her book *Basket of Blessings: 31 Days to a More Grateful Heart*, Karen O'Connor shares her experience with just such a practice. "If you want to be content, to experience peace," a friend had told Karen, "write down your blessings—the things you're grateful for—on slips of paper and put them in a container of some kind. A small basket or box or bag will do. Soon it will be full to overflowing. From time to time look at what you wrote. No one can be discontent for long with so much to be thankful for."

In addition to filling a "blessing basket" on a daily basis, we could write a letter to God once a year, listing all that pours out of our hearts for His extravagant grace to us. Think of what a joy it would be to keep our annual letters of gratitude to read through the years or to pass on to our children.

What a celebration we could have as we remind ourselves of the faithfulness of God.

Whether our thank-you moments are momentary, intentional pauses in the midst of a hectic day, thank-you notes to God for His many blessings, or lengthy discourses of His grace, cultivating an attitude of gratitude will remind us of the truth that undergirds our lives: "For the LORD is good and his love endures forever; his faithfulness continues through all generations" (Psalm 100:5).

Holidays like Thanksgiving, Christmas, and Easter can be joyful occasions, but I'm aware that they can be painful too. Perhaps you have lost a loved one, and this is the first time you will face a particular birthday or anniversary with an empty place at your table. Perhaps family times make you feel lonely, remind you of what's not true for you at this moment. I pray that you might know deep in your spirit that you belong to an eternal family; you are loved by God, enough for Him to send His precious Son to the cross for you. We have so much to celebrate as daughters of the King of kings. I pray that you might find a quiet place today to stop and lift your heart up in gratitude to our Father.

And just think, in Scotland we are told to eat our vegetables before we get dessert; here in America you get to do both at the same time.

You are loved!

— *Contagious Joy*

Finding Joy in a Cluttered-Up Sunset

● ● ● Thelma Wells

I know a woman who has gone through some rough times. Honey, I'm talkin' *really* rough times. Yet her faith is strong, and her attitude is joyful. One of her small pleasures is watching the sun go down in the evening. She calls herself a connoisseur of sunsets, and she has made this observation: a sunset—and a life—are richer, deeper, and more vibrant when there are clouds.

A sun that sets cleanly, without clouds, turns the sky a soft, pretty pink. That kind of sunset is okay but nothing special. In contrast, when there's a messy sky with patches of dark clouds hovering over the horizon to reflect back the full, glorious colors of the sunset, then the sky is streaked with a magnificent spectrum of incredible hues: deep purple, hot pink, velvety gray, flashing crimson, vivid violet, and dozens of other colors. That kind of sunset takes your breath away.

—Listen Up, Honey

Family Adjustments

● ● ● Sandi Patty

If I rise on the wings of the dawn,
if I settle on the far side of the sea, even there
your hand will guide me,
your right hand will hold me fast.
—Psalm 139:8–10

After Don and I married in Colorado with all our family and friends gathered around us, we stayed on in that beautiful Estes Park area for a few days of what we called our "familymoon," then we headed back to the Midwest, and while my kids spent a few days with their dad and Don's kids visited their mom in Michigan, Don and I moved all of his family's things into the big white house my kids and I had moved into after the divorce.

We wanted to make the actual moving-and-blending process as painless for the kids as possible, so by the time they came back, everything was settled, and Don's kids' things were moved to our house. New bunk beds were installed, my kids' clothes were moved around to accommodate the clothes that were coming in, toys and games were neatly arranged on shelves, and life in the blender began.

My kids—Anna, Jenni, Jonathan, and Erin—were now joined by Don's kids—Donnie, Aly, and Mollie. As the oldest child, Anna got her own room, which we had created by renovating the attic. Jenni also got to keep her own room, although it was a room the other kids had to pass through to get to the bathroom, so it wasn't all that private. Donnie, who had suddenly gone from oldest to middle child, shared a room and a set of bunk beds with Jonathan. And the three youngest girls—Aly, Mollie, and my Erin—shared a single bedroom.

For a while, everything was rosy. Then a few small skirmishes broke out, followed later by what sometimes sounded like a condensed replay of the Civil War. While there were plenty of peaceful and fun moments, specific rivalries quickly evolved. Although Donnie and Jonathan had been through a few unpleasant run-ins at school, their relationship flowed surprisingly well, and we were surprised that the loudest fighting occurred, not between the two boys, but between Donnie and Jenni. Somehow the two little eight-year-old dynamos managed to irritate each other by everything they did, beginning with breathing. Over the next few *years*, we would hear all sorts of yelling and screaming echoing down the staircase. A typical argument might sound like this.

"Mom! Donnie won't get out of my room. Make him get out!"

"Dad, she took my CD, the one I got in Michigan."

"This isn't your CD! This is mine. You loaned yours to Tommy."

This back-and-forth might go on a while, then we might hear a door slam or something hitting a wall, followed by, "Waaaaaaaaaaah!"

"Is there blood?" Don might ask, standing at the foot of the stairs.

"Yes!"

Although most of these incidents were resolved *without* bloodshed, there were a few times when someone was "accidentally" hit by flying debris or someone got pushed and . . .

Well, just let me say we *do* know the shortest route to the emergency room. Recently Jenn had to have some kind of medical exam, and she was told, "Oh! Your nose has been broken before." When she came home and told the family about it at dinner, she and Donnie argued about when it got broken and which one of their fights had caused it (although both incidents truly were accidents). Jenn said it happened "that time when we were fighting in the car."

"No, it was when we were arguing about what we were going to watch on TV," Donnie insisted. "*Twister* was coming on, and I was scared to watch it. I said turn it off. You said no, so we both ran for the clicker and I bumped you in the nose. I remember you had to stop the blood with one of Sam's diapers."

While Jenn and Donnie had some conflicts and felt confused and uncomfortable about the initial blending process, the three littlest girls seemed to do much better. Aly and Erin were six and five when Don and I got married, and they had become close while we were dating. As Aly says now, "At first it was like moving in with my best friend; it was fun, like one long party." Not that they didn't have their own squabbles occasionally as they adjusted from being best friends to becoming sisters. And then, as they got older and those adolescent hormones kicked in, there were more frequent spats. As Donnie says now with a weary sigh, "There were so many fights over whose bra it was."

And then there were the arguments over who sat where at the dinner table and who got to sit in the front seat of the minivan on the ride to school. Initially we had a rule that whoever got downstairs first each morning got the primo "shotgun" seat. But that caused too many knock-down-drag-out brawls on the staircase as two or more kids tried to edge out the others when they all got ready at the same time. Then

Donnie started getting up early and coming downstairs twenty minutes before time to leave so he could holler, "Shotgun!" and get the good seat—a situation that incited great resentment among those who, as a result of Donnie's promptness, *never* got to sit up front.

Things got so bad we eventually set up a "front-days" chart so each kid got a turn riding shotgun. It wasn't a simple chart, either, because there were too many kids and too few weekdays for each one to have a set day; i.e., Anna every Monday, Donnie every Tuesday.

Yes, many "adjustments" had to be made as we settled in together, but now, eleven years later, the yelling has pretty much stopped, and the kids have worked out a relationship that is, for the most part, harmonious. As Don says, "They argue, they fight, they fuss, but they also look out for each other and love each other. They're a family." It's interesting to me that some of our kids introduce each other now as "my stepsister" or "my stepbrother," but others, including Erin, and Anna, do not. "I stopped using *step* a long time ago," Aly says.

—*Life in the Blender*

Back-Alley Laughter

● ● ● Thelma Wells

*S*ister, when I tell you that hard times and messy rela-
tionships can help you appreciate your blessings
later on, you'd better believe me! Most people who know me
today will tell you I am a happy, joyful person, but I've known
some hard, hard times.

Granny Harrell raised me in a humble back-alley apartment, but it was a palace compared with the place my young,
disabled mother lived. When I visited her in the small tent she
had set up on a vacant lot, we slept together on a narrow cot.

Granny's husband, Daddy Harrell, babysat me while Granny
worked as a domestic for an aristocratic family. Whenever
Daddy Harrell couldn't watch me for some reason, I was sent to
the home of another relative who locked me in a dark, narrow
coat closet all day, saying that was the only way she could
make sure I was safe.

Hard times, for sure.

I know what it's like to watch a movie from the "colored
section" up in the balcony. I've waited at the backdoor of
restaurants, out by the garbage cans, to buy a hamburger
from businesses that wouldn't serve black people in the dining area. I attended segregated elementary and high schools,
was denied a spot in a business school because of my race,
and during college lived with four other African American
girls in a cubbyhole space in the dormitory basement next to

the boiler room. It was the only dorm room the university's black female students were allowed to occupy.

I've endured a broken heart, an empty bank account, and a serious health problem more times than I care to remember. But all those messes in my past—and those I may face in my future—just serve as the dark canvas that makes the bright happiness of my life today all the more noticeable, all the more precious.

You know, Jesus told us we would have trouble in this world (see John 16:33), and honey, He wasn't kidding! But He also said He would be with us through our troubles and bring us to a glorious reward. Repeatedly, He has already helped me turn my troubles into joy so that today my life is full and happy—and I'm still living here on old planet earth. Just imagine what kind of happiness He has in store for me when I move on to that grand family gathering up in heaven!

. . . .

—*Listen Up, Honey*

Life is an adventure. Hang on to your hat and
scream for all you're worth!

©2007 Barbara Johnson

Look for the Laugh

● ● ● Barbara Johnson

God will let you laugh again;
you'll raise the roof with shouts of joy.
—Job 8:21 MSG

*M*y friend Lynda loves to laugh more than just about anyone I know. She's 100 percent sanguine—full of joy, quick to laugh, and completely disorganized. That last characteristic tends to make Lynda a master at living amid the chaos caused by such things as lost phone numbers, forgotten names, and assorted machines and appliances she has no idea how to work. Such problems might drive other people crazy, but Lynda joyfully accepts these challenges as a normal part of life.

It's not unusual for her to call me, asking if I remember the name of her doctor and when her next appointment is. To be honest, I'm not that much better than she is at remembering such details, and with all the doctors and appointments I've had in the last few years since my cancer diagnosis, our conversations often go something like this:

"Barb, didn't I tell you I have a doctor's appointment sometime next week?"

"I seem to remember you said something about making one."

"Well, was it the doctor whose name starts with an *R* or a *W*? I can't remember."

"I thought you said you would be sure to remember this

time because this is the doctor that reminds you of a vege-table . . . or was he the one with the same name as an Old Testament prophet . . . ?"

"Hmmmm. I was thinking it was the doctor I see for my stomach trouble . . . or is this my appointment with the chiropractor?"

"Lynda, you really should write down these appointments!"

"Oh, Barb, I did write it down. But I lost the paper."

Life is always interesting when Lynda's around, because every day she loses something new—and while she's looking for it, she usually finds something old that she lost a month or a year ago. Every discovery prompts a gleeful celebration and another excited phone call to share her joy with me.

Lynda makes friends wherever she goes and always has a good story to tell about how that person helped, entertained, or inspired her, whether it's a street person who hangs out near the bookstore where she works or someone she meets in the doctor's waiting room.

Things haven't been easy for Lynda. She's endured heart-breaking loss and bottomless grief. But the thing about Lynda is, for all the things she loses in her everyday life, she can find the funny factor in any calamity. You can count on it. And Lynda's sister Terri has the same humor-hunting gift.

For instance, when Lynda and Terri were keeping vigil at their sweet mother's deathbed and they realized their mother was slipping away, Lynda leaned down and whispered, "Remember, Mommy, we'll meet at the eastern gate."

She was referring to a favorite gospel song about heaven that she and her mother loved to sing together. But at that time Terri had been living far away and didn't get to spend as much time with her mother as Lynda did, so she wasn't up to date on her mother's favorite hymns.

"What?" Terri exclaimed. "No one told me about meeting at the eastern gate. Who decided it would be the *eastern* gate? If nobody'd told me, I'd probably be waiting at the *western* gate, asking Jesus, 'Where *is* everybody?'"

Even as their hearts were breaking, the sisters laughed.

More recently, Terri asked Lynda if she could borrow the videotape of their parents' fiftieth anniversary party, which had been held many years earlier. Terri wanted to show her husband all the friends and relatives they hadn't seen for many years. Several of the people on the tape had died since the anniversary, and Terri wanted to see them again. Plus, she thought it would be fun for her and her husband to see their kids when they were little. Of course Lynda obliged. Then, a few days later, came the dreaded phone call.

"Oh, Lynda, something awful has happened."

"What, Terri? Are you okay" Lynda asked.

"Oh, Lynda, it's so awful I can't stand it. It's terrible. It's horrible. It's . . ."

"Terri, is everyone all right? Has anyone died?"

"Lynda, you know Mom and Dad's anniversary tape? Well . . . I taped over it."

"Terri, how *could* you!" Lynda shrieked. "That's the only copy! Oh, I can't believe you did that."

Both sisters were crying, and then Lynda remembered something she had heard a comedian say not too long ago: "If all you've got is pain, then all you've got is pain. But if you can laugh, then you can use the pain to make your life better."

Choking back sobs, Lynda said, "Terri, stop crying. We have to think of something to laugh at, or this whole thing will just be pain. Think of something, Terri—quick."

Terri paused and then said, "Well, Lynda, you know how I've always wanted you to watch that show *Reba*? Well, now you can."

And then they laughed. And as they laughed they thought of reasons why the tape wasn't all that important anyway: most of the people on the tape were old people, and their kids wouldn't know who the old people were, and the like.

"We have our memories, and that's better than any old videotape anyway," Lynda said.

"Yes, but you know, your memory's been slipping lately."

"Oh, who cares?" Lynda replied. "It's not like we'll never see those people again—we'll see most of them in heaven."

For nearly twenty years, Lynda has been my close friend and devoted encourager. What a blessing she has been to me, always bringing with her the gift of laughter whenever she calls or visits.

One day she brought a magazine clipping that described a weight-control plan she thought would make me laugh. According to this method, doctors have you swallow a balloon that is then inflated inside your stomach to make you feel full so you don't want to eat.

The thing that made us laugh was the balloon's removal system. It had a string attached to it that would snake back up your esophagus and hang out your nose! Lynda and I had the best time brainstorming about how it would be to have that string hanging out our noses—and all the answers we could give to explain what it was to the people who asked: "Oh this? I just pull it to turn on the light in my brain. You know, whenever I want to have a light-bulb moment." Or we could tie a bead to the end of the string and make a fashion statement, or we could just stuff the string back up into our nostrils so it was out of sight, at least until we sneezed.

Lynda and I have shared a lot of laughs over the years, and that laughter has been a lifeline that has saved me from the cesspool of misery many times. It's also provided fodder for some of my writing, including the time I called her and said, "Oh, Lynda, I hope you won't be mad at me. I wrote about your bra in my new book." (She'd shown up at my house one day looking especially sharp, and when I commented on how good she looked, she confessed she was wearing a new bra called Nobody's Perfect. That just *had* to go into one of my books!)

In addition to laughter, Lynda and I have also shared a strong, unwavering faith in God, who gives us both tears and laughter. Despite the challenges we've faced, we've come out on the other side with the same attitude as the Old Testament character Hannah. She was tormented for years by her childlessness, and when the Lord answered her plea for a child, Hannah prayed, "The LORD has filled my heart with joy. . . . I can laugh at my enemies; I am glad because you have helped me!" (1 Samuel 2:1 NCV).

For Hannah, the enemies were her barrenness and the women who scoffed at her because of it. For me, the enemies have been such things as grief and loss, cancer and diabetes. But despite those hardships, God has given me laughter-loving friends like Lynda, and He has "filled my heart with joy."

He'll do the same for you. Ask Him to help you find the laughter in the painful problems you face. Ask Him to send you a friend whose heart is so full of joy it splashes over onto you. Laugh with her at every opportunity, and if the opportunity doesn't readily present itself . . . hunt it down!

And then *be* that kind of friend to someone else.

. . . .

—*Contagious Joy*

Being a Friend, Even When It Hurts

● ● ● Jan Silvious

O ne of the greatest joys in life is friendship. I love this quote from our country's colonial times: "A true friend unbosoms freely, advises justly, assists readily, adventures boldly, takes all patiently, defends courageously, and continues a friend unchangeably" (William Penn).

The most important aspect of friendship is doing what is best for your friend even when it hurts you.

. . . .

—Big Girls Don't Whine

Bringing Your Pity Party to a Screeching Halt

● ● ● Thelma Wells

The LORD is my strength and my song;
he has become my salvation.
—Exodus 15:2

Perhaps you read bumper stickers on the backs of vehicles as I do. One day when I was broke, bummed out, and disgusted, I was having a major pity party while driving down the freeway. In front of me was a truck with a bumper sticker that displayed in large letters, "Life is tough, and then you die." Not what I wanted to hear that day. No, the "adventure" of having only twenty-five cents in my pocket, nothing in the bank, and no sweepstakes possibilities in view was about to drive me to my wits' end.

My pity party got more raucous with every passing second. Whimpering and gasping for breath, I noticed lights flashing on an automobile dealership sign just ahead. I almost couldn't believe my eyes when I got close enough to read: "Tough times don't last. Tough people do!" This sign was flashing on the watts of a whole different current. A second ago I was dying; instantly after reading Dr. Robert Schuller's famous words, I'd become a "tough" person who understood that "this, too, shall pass." My pity party came to a screeching halt.

I learned a lot from that little drive. Life is full of experiences that challenge, confound, and concern us—and create circumstances that cause the road in front of us to take turns we don't anticipate or welcome. We get news we didn't want and can't send back by overnight mail. Family situations are strained. We feel as though even our best friends don't understand what we're going through. Life feels so tough sometimes that we wish we were dead. I know. I've been there.

But I've also been there for the resurrection moments. Just when I feel that I can't take one more second in the black hole of my own hope-starved soul, God shows up in ways I don't anticipate. I get "zapped" by a jolt of encouragement on the side of the road. I turn over a rock in the path and discover a treasure instead of more torment. I get to the bottom of the barrel and find out there's a way of escape. The bottom drops out and I land in the palm of God's hand.

> For God, who said, "Let light shine out of darkness," made his light shine in our hearts to give us the light of the knowledge of the glory of God in the face of Christ.
>
> But we have this treasure in jars of clay to show that this all-surpassing power is from God and not from us. We are hard pressed on every side, but not crushed; perplexed, but not in despair; persecuted, but not abandoned; struck down, but not destroyed. We always carry around in our body the death of Jesus, so that the life of Jesus may also be revealed in our body. (2 Corinthians 4:6–10)

If that's not a powerful description of what adventure is all about in the life of a believer, then I don't know what is. I don't naturally welcome being hard-pressed, perplexed, or persecuted any more than you do. But when the dark experiences of life come knocking at my door, I am promised that light will be provided in the midst of my bewilderment. And not just any light, but the glorious spiritual light that only the presence of Christ can give. When the going gets tough and I feel like death warmed over, in my very worst moment of misery the bright light and life of Jesus can be revealed. In the glow of His presence my whole attitude can shift instantaneously. A miracle!

I believe that's what I experienced when my road seemed so overwhelmingly rough and dark that day on the freeway. In one moment I was absolutely convinced that the message in front of me was true: "Life is tough, and then you die." No hope. No point. No adventure. But just up the road was a little fork on my right—a blinking, dazzling truth I'd completely forgotten as my pity party kicked into high gear: "Tough times don't last. Tough people do."

You are tough because the Spirit of God lives in you—and if anyone tells you otherwise, you want to meet them outside. Whether things are good or bad, happy or sad, difficult or easy, you're in the middle of a God-ordained adventure that changes day by day—sometimes second by second. You are never abandoned, never destroyed. When the going gets tough, the tough in Christ get going because God is faithful. Embracing an adventuresome life in spite of life's ups and downs requires a knowledge of God's ways, faith in His promises, a belief in His goodness and love, and a choice to live moment by moment under His grace.

Look up for a moment from whatever you're focused on and notice what may be just beyond your sight. Keep moving forward, and you'll see a beacon of hope at the next fork in the road.

—*The Great Adventure Devotional*

God's E-mail

● ● ● Marilyn Meberg

One day God was looking down at earth and saw the result of the outrageously bad choices His creation was making. He decided to send down an angel to do a little research.

When the angel returned, he reported that 95 percent of the people were behaving badly and 5 percent were not. God was not pleased, so He decided to e-mail the 5 percent who were behaving well and commend them for their good choices.

Do you know what that e-mail said?

Just wondering, because I didn't get one either.

—Freedom Inside and Out

Part 3

Is This Funny, or Am I Losing My Mind?

Trying to Remember Why We're Laughing

• • • • •

Of all the things I've lost,
I miss my mind the most.

Brain Fractures

● ● ●   Patsy Clairmont

Know what fractures my brain? Numbers. Somehow they just don't tally for me.

It makes me nervous just saying the word *math*. Or worse yet, *algebra*. (Isn't that a type of undergarment?) Or what about *metrics*? Eek!

Any numerical word can cause me to hyperventilate. Numbers just don't stick in my brain, not even with superglue. When someone asks me how old I am and I pause before answering, it may seem like I'm in denial; but truth is, I forget. And I hate to say, "Just a second; I'll check my driver's license." Or, "Wait a minute; I'll ask my kids." Nor do I feel comfortable just confessing, "I don't know," for fear they'll call the Old-Age Patrol.

Age is so fluctuating. I mean, it just keeps switching on me. If my age would stay the same for, say, a decade at a time, it would really help.

Once, I told a fellow who had asked my age that I was 85–43. He stared at me like he thought my cranium was cracked.

My mind was intact; it was my numbers I had flip-flopped. I had inadvertently given him my address . . . from three houses ago. Well, at least I didn't give him my Social Security number.

I blame my number dilemma on the multiplication tables. They messed me up. Honestly, I was doing fine in school until I had to multiply. Adding and subtracting were fairly friendly, but multiplying was hostile from the get-go. I spent untold hours being drilled on the multiplication tables via flashcards by my more-than-determined mom. I promise you, even using a high-powered drill (and my mom was), I still can't say my nines.

And if multiplying weren't bad enough, then I had to learn fractions. I say, if it's a fraction of anything, why bother? Get over the small stuff. Just dust it away and keep moving. That way, nobody gets hurt.

Have you noticed how many numbers we are required to know to function in society? Sooner rather than later, folks ask us either to take a number, number off, or spout a list of digits the breadth of North America: address, zip code, telephone number, age, date of birth, Social Security number, P.O. box, license plate number, driver's license number, hotel room, the time, combination lock, today's date, families' dates of birth, PIN, security system code, shoe size, frequent-flyer number, height, and weight (like I'm telling that!). No wonder people *punch* time clocks—they're angry that they've had to deal with one more set of numbers!

When I grew up, I thought I wanted to punch a clock as a bookstore owner, but God protected my prospective customers and me because He knew I would need to know more than how to read a book—I'd have to know how to keep the books. I can't even handle the cash register, much less balance columns of figures. My idea of balancing books is holding one in each hand. And inventory? Just call in the white coats. My eyes glaze over when I see shelves laden with anything that I might have to compute.

For years I wasn't certain God meant for us to mess with numbers, but then I remembered Noah, who had to count the animals. Not a job I'd want. I've seen those pictures of all the animals agreeably lining up and filing aboard the ark, but I don't buy it. I think they were squirming, nipping, bucking, and hiding. I think loading that ark put stretch marks on Noah's grace. Have you ever tried to count rooting pigs, hysterical hyenas, or hot-flashing penguins? And who can keep track of numbers with trumpeting elephants, screeching monkeys, and squawking parrots? Don't you just know the donkeys sat down on the gangplank more than once and refused to budge, jamming the count? No, make me a greeter at Wal-Mart where I nod and "Howdy-ya-do?" the folks coming aboard, but don't make me calculate anything.

The Lord has instructed us to "number our days." I am on day 21,763. Or so I think. No one is here to check my math. I wouldn't even try to figure it out, except the Lord asks me to, so It must be important. Maybe it's a type of righteous reality check. Sort of a "Here's what I've given you thus far, what have you done with it?"

Why don't you grab a pencil and jot in the margin what day you're on? Go ahead, it's all right to use your calculator.

—*All Cracked Up*

The Limpings of the Well-Intended and Misinformed

● ● ● Marilyn Meberg

> God deliberately chose things the
> world considers foolish in order to shame
> those who think they are wise.
> —1 Corinthians 1:27 NLT

I was heading out for food reinforcements and offered to pick up a few things for Luci. She gave me a list.

Forty minutes later I knocked on her door with her bag of items. As I spread them out on her counter, we both became quiet and simply stared. There were two packages of Twinkies, two cans of Ajax, one bottle of mouthwash guaranteed to remove plaque, an easy-pour bottle of Lysol deodorizing cleaner that cuts grease and disinfects, and an eight-ounce can of Bud Lite.

Her response to this bewildering array of items, which I did not remember picking out, putting in my basket, or paying for, was, "Marilyn, the only thing I can use here is the can of Bud Lite" (she was kidding, of course).

"Well, but I have no idea where this stuff came from. I must have scooped someone else's items up and left them with mine. Someone in Frisco is going to open their bag and find vanilla yogurt, white cheddar cheese, unsalted wheat thin crackers, and a package of Hefty garbage bags."

After a thoughtful silence, Luci said, " What about my eggs?"

"You didn't have eggs on your list."

"No, and I didn't have Bud Lite on there either!"

It would be fun to tell you about the times some of us Women of Faith speakers missed our flight departures because we misread our tickets, or left a jacket wadded on the plane seat next to us, or mistakenly put a restaurant spoon in "our" purse to be discovered later when searching for the evening niacin pills.

"How did the spoon get in the purse?"

"Beats me."

"Me, too."

How could my friends and I misread a flight schedule, leave a jacket wadded in seat 21B on American flight 2021, buy Bud Lite instead of eggs, or stick a spoon in our purse that belongs to Texas Land and Cattle restaurant? These are the limpings of the well intended and misinformed, but I am endlessly and joyfully encouraged by it all.

It seems to me that God has a special place for those crea-tures and persons who cannot live up to the cardinal standard of excellence. Read this passage from 1 Corinthians 1:26–29 and see if you too don't feel better about your occasional limps:

> Remember, dear brothers and sisters, that few of you were wise in the world's eyes, or powerful, or wealthy when God called you. Instead, God deliberately chose things the world considers foolish in order to shame those who think they are wise. And he chose those who are powerless to shame those who are powerful. God chose things despised by the world, things counted as nothing at all, and used them to bring to nothing what the world considers important, so that no one can ever boast in the presence of God. (NLT)

—Contagious Joy

If Only I Had a Brain . . .

● ● ● Ann Luna

Just a note to send my greetings,
Let you know I'm still alive,
Though I'm getting more forgetful.
Things just seem to slip my mind.

I fuss and fret and try to think,
But all that comes to me
Is pain between my eyeballs—
My head hurts terribly!

I walk into the bathroom
To retrieve a headache pill.
There I stand, listing my options,
Wondering what I'm doing here.

I back into the hallway,
"Start all over," I suggest.
Then, remembering what I needed,
I head back toward the shelf.

But once more, memory fails me.
"Why am I here?" I ask.
Then my eye falls on my toothbrush,
And I take my dentures out.

Still, it seems like there was something else . . .
"What could it be?" I pose.
Then I fill the tub with water
And sit down awhile to soak.

"This isn't it," I tell myself.
"I came for something more."
Then I spy the scales and, dripping wet,
Stride quickly 'cross the floor.

I step onto the circular disk
And struggle hard to see
The number on the dial below—
"Where *could* my glasses be?"

I step into the bedroom
Where I'm sure my specs I'll find.
But standing there beside the bed,
I just cannot decide

Why I've come here—did the phone ring?
Then I see the looking glass.
Good heavens! I'm stark naked!
I'd better get dressed—fast!

I step up to the closet,
Pull the chain to flick the light.
My nightgown hangs before me.
"Oh! It's time to say good night."

I slip into my nightie
As I hum a sleep-tight song,

Pull the covers up around me—
But wait! There's something wrong.

It's the sun. It's at my window!
How could day arrive so soon?
Then I spy the clock and blink my eyes.
"For heaven's sake! It's noon!"

I hurry to the bathroom,
Since I'm running far behind.
There I stand, listing my options,
Wondering what I came to find.

I see this note I started—
Now I can't remember when.
"I'll finish it, right now, right here—
If I can find a pen."

I shuffle to the kitchen,
Where by chance I come upon
A recipe for turnips.
But, my stars! The type is small.

I squint and try to read it,
But my focus is so bad,
A pain streaks o'er my temples,
Creates misery in my head.

I walk into the bathroom
To retrieve a simple pill . . .
It all seems so familiar—
What AM I doing here?

Are You the One?

● ● ● Barbara Johnson

> Don't be afraid! Stand still and you will see
> the LORD save you today.
> —Exodus 14:13 NCV

*D*ear Barbara,
Lately I have had several fears that I may be going off my rocker. How can I know if this is what is happening to me?

Fearful in Fayetteville

Dear Fearful,

We know that one out of every four people in this country is mentally unbalanced. So, you just think of your three closest friends. . . . If they seem to be okay, then you're the one!

God can use reversals to move us forward.

. . . .

—*Daily Splashes of Joy*

© 2004 Randy Glasbergen. www.glasbergen.com

"Actually, I only come here to lie down.
I can't get any rest at home!"

It's Gotta Be Here Somewhere

● ● ● Martha Bolton

D o you realize the average person loses up to six weeks every year looking for things that he or she has misplaced at work—files, pens, computer disks, the boss.

We lose things at home, too. We misplace our glasses, car keys, slippers, remote control, checkbook, wallet, hairbrush, pens, and pencils.

When we finally find the missing item, it's often in the strangest of places. Like when we discover we put a cucumber in our purse and our cell phone in the vegetable drawer of the refrigerator.

And has this ever happened to you? You're in the middle of looking for something when you forget what it was you were looking for. Now, you would think that this would take the stress off finding the lost item. After all, if you can't remember what you lost, it stands to reason that you would no longer worry about having lost it. But that's not how it works. Forgetting what you're looking for only makes matters worse. You stress even more because you know you lost something, and the longer it takes you to find it, the more valuable you're sure it was.

When you figure we're wasting six weeks of our lives looking for articles we lose at work and at least that much time looking for things we lose at home, maybe we should try to do something about it. Maybe we could all benefit from signing up for one of those memory seminars. Haven't you wondered what goes on at them? Do they serve ginseng-spiked punch and sit around playing Pin the Tail on the Whatchamacallit?

I saw a helpful product in a catalog recently. It was an electronic locator. It came with four different pagers that would send a beeping sound to whatever item it was programmed to find. Pretty ingenious. I bought two sets. One set to use for the four items, and another set to locate the pagers for when I lose *them*.

I'm sure you've done this, too—gotten into your car, driven off, and totally forgotten that you had set something on the roof. That's always exciting, isn't it? Soda cans, your briefcase, mail, pizza. You don't realize it until you're on the freeway going seventy miles per hour and you see someone passing you waving their arms frantically. By the time you figure out that those lips being whipped in the wind are mouthing "Pizza on the roof," the pepperoni is already sliding down your windshield.

Memory loss isn't all bad, though. There are some positive things that can come out of it. If you can't remember your outstanding bills, you have a lot more spending money. If you can't recall people's names, you have a whole bunch of new friendships to make and enjoy. And if you can't remember your embarrassing moments, what's to keep you from the fun of making more?

....

—*I Think, Therefore I Have a Headache*

Learning the Hard Way

● ● ● Thelma Wells

A Sunday school teacher once said she'd told herself she would never, ever pray for patience again. "Every time I've asked God to help me learn to be more patient, He's helped me learn, all right. But I've had to learn the hard way! I pray for patience, and the next thing I know I'm in some long, torturous ordeal with no way out of it and just one way through It. The only choice I have is to force myself to be patient—or lose my mind."

. . . .

—Listen Up, Honey

The Joyful Trickster

● ● ● Marilyn Meberg

A number of years ago I was indulging in one of my favorite taste treats at a small sandwich shop that also specializes in varieties of yogurt. One of my favorites is peanut butter yogurt. Now that may not sound very appealing to you, but listen to this! I slather the yogurt with raspberry topping made from frozen raspberries, and then top it off with a generous sprinkling of chopped peanuts. I was just settling my spoon into this wonderful concoction late one morning, when the door of the shop opened suddenly and a tiny, elderly lady burst through it. She scanned the shop for a second and then darted over to my table, pulled out the chair across from me, and sat down. Before I had quite grasped what was happening, she leaned across the table and whispered, "Is anyone following me?" I looked suspiciously behind her and out into the parking lot from which she had emerged and whispered back, "No—there's no one in sight!"

"Good," she said, and with that she slipped out her teeth, snapped open her purse, and dropped the teeth into its depths.

Throughout this unexpected scene my spoon had remained frozen between my dish and my mouth. Galvanized into action by the melting of my yogurt, I put the spoon in my mouth; the little lady fixed her eyes upon my spoon and then upon my dish. I asked if she had ever eaten peanut butter yogurt with raspberry sauce. Without ever looking at me, she said that she had wanted to try it all her life but never had. I calculated that "all her life" was probably some eighty to eighty-five years. That seemed a long time to live without peanut butter yogurt. I asked her if she'd like me to get her some. Without a moment's hesitation, she said yes but still never took her eyes off my yogurt. By the time I returned to our table with her order, she was nearly halfway through my dish of yogurt! I found this amusing, especially since she offered no apology or explanation for taking my food. I started eating what would have been hers and we slurped our way along in companionable silence.

Across the street from where we were eating is an establishment for senior citizens that ranges in care for those in fairly good health but need watching, to those in poor health needing constant attention. I classified my little eating companion as an escapee from this home. The minute she finished her yogurt, she began rapid preparations to leave. She whisked her teeth out from the bottom of her purse, popped them in place, and jumped up, heading for the door. Concerned about her crossing the busy intersection alone, I asked if she'd let me accompany her. She was out the door and into the parking lot so fast I had to almost run to keep up with her. She never granted permission for me to go with her, but I trotted along anyway. As I had surmised, she made her way into the senior citizens' building and scurried down the hall. The only thing she said to me was that she had to hurry or she'd miss lunch.

I stopped at the nurses' station and asked the girl behind the counter if she had noticed the little lady I had come with. She said, "Oh yes. That's Felisha; she's a real live wire." Then she asked if I happened to be a relative. I told her Felisha and I had just met at the sandwich shop less than an hour ago.

The girl's eyes sparkled as she asked, "Did you by any chance buy her a dish of peanut butter yogurt?" I was a bit startled as I admitted I had. The girl laughed and told me Felisha knew every trick in the book.

As I walked back to my car, my admiration for Felisha grew with each step. What a deal she had going for her. Who wouldn't succumb to the plight of a little, elderly refugee from a retirement home who had always wanted to taste peanut butter yogurt but had never been given the opportunity? Several weeks later I went to ask Felisha if she'd go with me to get some yogurt. When I asked for the location of her room, the girl at the desk informed me that Felisha had died in her sleep several nights before. At first I felt a deep pang of remorse as I visualized that energetic lady and the short but delightful interaction I had experienced with her. However, as I crawled into my Fiat to leave, that remorse gave way to a strong feeling of elation. What a way to go. Not only did she have the enviable experience of drifting quietly from this world, but right up to the end, she entered into the simple joys in life—simple joys like peanut butter yogurt slathered in raspberry sauce, smothered with chopped peanuts and paid for by someone else.

—*Choosing the Amusing*

Doing and Being

● ● ● Luci Swindoll

ot long ago I was in a local bookstore, investigating one of the many new books on dieting, and discovered there was an entire diet section in the store. It was full of overweight people, lethargically pulling the volumes from the shelves and leafing through pages of information pertaining to newer and better ways to take off inches and pounds. A few were talking about that four-letter word which seems to dominate the English language—DIET.

And that isn't all. In the aisle next to the one where we were solving the problems of the *avoirdupois*, there were three ladies poring over a new book on exercise . . . running, I believe it was. They looked fabulous. Tan. Thin. Sleek. Perfect. Yet, they confessed to one another their desire to run at least one more mile next time . . . to get an even richer tan . . . to work out at the club more faithfully. All of our team in the diet section were trying not to listen as they rehearsed their goals, since they, no doubt, were already outdistancing us in every way. I simply resumed munching my Almond Joy.

After locating the book I was seeking, I picked it up and started toward the cash register. On my way, I walked through an aisle labeled MENTAL HEALTH. These publications ranged from books on transcendental meditation to a volume entitled *Mental Gymnastics—Exercising While You Wait*. The person holding a copy of that appeared as though he were. His eyes were closed and I was certain he was either in a trance or not among the living, when suddenly, his eyes popped open and he realized I was looking straight at him. "Oh, I'm not doing a gymnastic," he said. "My contacts are killing me and I was trying to rest my eyes." We exchanged a few lines about the price we all pay for vanity, then we parted, the same strangers we were when we met.

On my way back to work I started thinking about all the books that must have been written on health. Countless thousands. And not only books! Good health is touted on television, radio, and in films. National magazines are replete with recommended ways to be healthy and stay healthy. Of course, we all know why. Health is a treasure and fitness is an enviable state for anyone. When we have healthy minds, bodies, and spirits, we have personal assurance that we will be strong enough and sound enough to live our lives fully, coping effectively with life's problems rather than becoming the victim of them.

But few things in life are ideal. Realistically, therefore, we must admit that the living of daily life produces all sorts of inner factions and tensions that can manifest themselves in physical pain, mental anguish, and spiritual depression. Surely, no one has trouble admitting that! That's the way things are. But . . . as we grasp good principles for healthy living, as we learn that we can prevent certain ills from occurring by simply using our heads, and as we realize that God provides marvelous promises for His children to claim and rely on when we are not well, the prognosis for a sound and healthy life becomes brighter and more probable.

However, to achieve this kind of thinking and to live on this plane, one must DO certain things to provide physical well-being, and BE certain ways to maintain the homeostasis required for one's psyche. I have hanging on the wall of my office a clever saying that reminds me of this need for balance between doing and being:

To DO IS TO BE—Plato

To BE IS TO DO—Sartre

To DO BE DO BE DO—Sinatra

I think Ol' Blue Eyes had the best outlook of all, don't you?

. . . .

—*Wide My World, Narrow My Bed*

My Little Chickadee

● ● ● Marilyn Meberg

I love the story of an elderly couple who enjoyed having younger couples over for dinner. They liked to bridge the generation gap and usually had fun in the process. During one of those dinners, a young husband noted how gracious and loving the old man was to his wife, calling her "Doll Face," "Darling," "Honey," and "Pumpkin."

While "Pumpkin" was in the kitchen getting coffee, the young man said, "I'm impressed with your love for your wife. I think it's wonderful that after all these years you call her those loving pet names."

"I have to tell you the truth," the old man responded. "About ten years ago I forgot her name."

. . . .

—*Irrepressible Hope*

Cleaning Up after the Chaos

● ● ● Sandi Patty

After all the work Don and I had done to prepare the kids—all the talks we'd had and the time we'd shared with them before our marriage—we were shell-shocked to hear how they remembered the actual blending process. To hear them tell it, we did everything wrong!

The surprises continued in another session when the topic of family meetings was brought up. Frankly, I considered these frequent gatherings one of the cornerstones of our successful family life. I started organizing them with just my four kids after I came back from my stay at the residential therapy center, where I had learned how valuable it is for everyone in a group (or a family) to check in from time to time and make sure everyone knows what's going on and has a safe place to air any issues or grievances.

So my assessment of our family meetings is that they've always worked quite well, and Don agrees with me. On the other hand, here's how our conversation went when the kids were describing them:

Anna: Mom or Don gets on the intercom and says, "Come down right now for a family meeting!" And immediately you hear someone say, "Oh, can I please be excused?" And then someone else says, "Me too!" and "Yeah, can I be excused too?"

Okay, this is Sandi again. I just want to say in my defense that if I'm calling a family meeting that night, I usually put a note on the kitchen bulletin board that morning notifying everyone of the family meeting, and I also remind the kids as they're leaving for school.

Jenn: We don't enjoy family meetings. Sometimes they're about nothing.

Anna: And there are the individual "meetings," when you hear, "Anna, I need to see you a minute in the living room." And then they'll add, "You're not in trouble."

Donnie: And then when they *don't* say that, you think, *Oh, boy*. I think I had the most trips to the living room of anyone.

Jenn: That was the bad-news room. If they called you in there, you knew there was something bad going on.

Anna: But a regular, all-family meeting is in the kitchen. It usually takes a long time for everyone to gather, and some of us get tired of waiting and drift back to what we were doing, so there are lots of calls on the intercom.

Mom is usually the one who has the agenda about whatever topic we're supposed to discuss. Maybe it's something like this year's family vacation—where and when we're going to go. Mom will throw out the choices or ask a question when we're all finally sitting around the kitchen table; the majority of us are doodling on the calendar she printed out for us. Of course, this may be the one time this week that we've all been together, so we're talking and joking and laughing.

Pretty soon, Mom will quietly say, "Well, if no one's going to talk about it, I'll talk to myself."

Then Don will give us a fifteen-minute lecture on how we need to respect Mom and give her our attention. As soon as Don starts talking, Donnie starts cracking jokes, and we all start laughing again. Then Don says, "You know what, Sandi? I just feel like we might as well go upstairs and talk to ourselves, because no one here is listening."

So maybe Don leaves. Then the cleaning begins. Mom

starts cleaning, and she cleans very forcefully so we can all hear the cleaning happening. She's loading the dishwasher or emptying the dishwasher and rattling those dishes and slamming those cabinet doors. Then she starts wiping the counters like she's going to scrub the tops right off of them.

● ● ●

I have to admit that I laughed along with everyone else as the kids were reliving what it's like in our family meetings. And I also have to admit that when something irritates me, I start cleaning. I tend to wear my feelings on my sleeve, and I also try to think of every possible ramification of a decision before it's made. But since nobody can do that, invariably I miss something. And I just hate that.

Let's say I've called a family meeting to discuss possible vacation places and dates, and someone will say, "I don't know . . . none of those times really work for me. I thought you knew I had yada-yada-yada then, Mom."

Then I'll get really quiet, devastated that I hadn't remembered that potential scheduling conflict. Everyone else is moving on to other topics, the vacation plan is out the window, and I'm taking it all very personally. That's when I start cleaning.

I know it's strange, but it's the way I am. Just sharing my testimony, as my friend Chonda Pierce would say.

. . . .

—Life in the Blender

Are You Talking to Yourself Again?

● ● ● Thelma Wells

*G*irl, do you talk to yourself? Do you ask yourself questions? Do you answer those questions? Do you interrupt yourself before you get an answer? If you do, you're in good company. Some of the best decisions you can make are between you and yourself. Most people who talk to themselves are not crazy; they're at least talking to someone intelligent for a change. So, it's fine to talk to yourself if you're saying the right things.

The wrong way to talk to yourself is to talk down to yourself.

Refrain from saying things like, "I can't do anything right." "What's wrong with me?" "I am so stupid." "I can't get anywhere on time." "Things just don't work out right for me." "I'm sick and tired of being sick and tired." "They don't like me." "I'm such a loser." "People are always jerking me around." "I hate this." "Trouble just seems to find me." "I don't care what happens." "Life is hard and then you die."

Do not say these negative things to yourself. No! No! No!

What you put into your mind will settle in your spirit and come out of your mouth. Don't even think about it, Girl. Change the way you talk to *you*.

I believe in affirmations. An affirmation is a positive statement spoken in first-person singular, present tense, as if it had already happened. Here are some affirmations. Repeat them after me:

"I like myself."

"Things work out well for me."

"I am attractive and charming."

"I enjoy life."

"I am blessed."

"I am healthy."

"I am appreciated."

"I enjoy rest and relaxation."

"I like people."

"I am successful."

"I am progressing in my career."

"I love my family."

"I have wonderful friends."

"I cherish the gift of life."

"I have all the money I need to do whatever I want."

Now, stop laughing. If you keep saying it and working toward it, you'll make room in your life for God to make it all come true.

Baby, it is so important to speak to yourself positively! I read somewhere that your body will follow where your mind leads. What I mean by all this is, when you change your focus from the negatives about you to the positives about you, you refocus your attention away from what's bringing you down to what can bring you up.

— *Girl, Have I Got Good News for You*

Pondering Backward

● ● ● Luci Swindoll

*I*n my younger years, I wish I had spent less time waiting for someone to ask me for answers and more time being willing to listen to those who had lived long enough to actually know some of the answers. If I had listened more, then I surely would have learned more—about life, about others, and about myself. And as I learned from others by really listening to them, then I would have been able to laugh more, because let's face it: funny stuff happens in life. Although I didn't listen or learn nearly enough in my younger years, I did learn to laugh. And as I stepped back to laugh at life and myself and situations, I was finally able to fully and freely love—to love God, to love who He created me to be, and to love all the people God has sent to enrich my life.

If God gives you a long life, one day you'll be my age (or perhaps you are now). You'll then take time to look backward too. Your brain will simply ponder the past whether you want it to or not.

You'll have regrets and disappointments. You'll remember sorrows you bore and temptations you failed to overcome. You'll smile when you consider joyful adventures and risks that catapulted you into achievement. You might even find tears welling up because of a loved one lost along the way or a dream that never materialized. You'll feel grateful for the fact God never let you down and for His severe mercy that taught you lessons you could have never learned unless your heart was broken.

All of that is life.

. . . .

—Life! Celebrate It

Part 4

Family Funnies

Laughing with Our Loved Ones

• • • • •

The best time to put the children to bed is
while you still have the strength.
—Croft M. Pentz

The Big Day

● ● ● Sheila Walsh

Saturday, December 3, was a beautiful day. I woke up
to sunshine streaming through the windows of my
room at Charleston's Meeting Street Inn. That night this
same luxurious bedroom would be our honeymoon suite.

I looked at my dress, hanging on the outside of the
wardrobe.

It was so beautiful! I knew I would feel like a fairy princess
in it. I was so happy! I had a shower and put on jeans and a
sweater and went for a walk. The wedding ceremony was at
four in the afternoon, so I had time to wander.

At noon I met my mom and Frances at the beauty salon
We all got wedding hairdos and had our makeup done. My
mom never wears much makeup—a little foundation, powder,
and a touch of blush. She doesn't wear lipstick or eye makeup.
I told the girl to give her the works. She looked beautiful.

The limousine arrived for me at 3:30. I had my gown in a
garment bag so I could change at the church. When the car
pulled up outside St. Matthew's Lutheran Church, I struggled
out of the door with my bags and gown. Then I saw Eleanor.
She looked at me with a strange, dazed expression. Realizing
how difficult it was for me to carry a poofy, Cinderella wedding gown with everything else, she started to come toward
me. Then she said, "Oh no, I can't. I'm just like a zombie," and
went inside.

I had no idea what she was talking about. The limo driver helped me inside, and then I asked him to go check on my mother-in-law-to-be.

The bridesmaids and I had so much fun getting ready. My matron of honor, Nancy Goudie, had been my best friend since I was sixteen. She had flown over from the United Kingdom for the wedding. I had four bridesmaids and two darling blonde-haired, twin flower girls. We all laughed and talked as we fixed each other's hair. Then Eleanor fell through the door of the dressing room like the survivor of a train wreck.

"Mom, what's wrong?" I asked, as she sank into a chair.

"It's all a mess," she said. "It's all going wrong! It's a disaster!"

"What's going wrong?" I asked Eleanor as I fetched a glass of water for her.

"Your father-in-law has no bow tie!"

I tried not to laugh. She had worked so hard, so very hard to make this the perfect day she had always imagined, and the rental place had forgotten Pop's bow tie, which apparently was a bad omen to her.

"Mom, that's all right. Someone can lend him one. Don't worry. It'll be okay. There are no bad omens, just bad hairdos . . . God's here. We'll be fine."

We all tried to settle her down.

Then it was time. My thoughts turned to my dad. He died when I was four years old, but at moments like these I missed him as acutely as if he had died the week before. Yet my brother, Stephen, was standing at the back of the church with me, and he was now the age my dad was when he died. It seemed like a gift to have him there. That's how Stephen has always seemed to me, a gift.

Sounds of my homeland filled the air. A lone bagpipe player piped the mothers down the aisle, playing my mother's favorite Scottish melody. Then it was my turn. As I walked toward Barry on the arm of my brother, I could have skipped. I could have run. I was so happy!

During the ceremony, Barry and I took communion. He seemed restless at my side, wishing it were over. Finally we walked down the aisle together and were off to the reception at the Charleston Society Hall. A blur! A beginning. A wonderful beginning. That's all I could think of.

The band we had hired was double booked, so they had sent a backup. They were so bad, it was hilarious. The trumpet player had the worst toupee I'd ever seen; it looked as if he'd killed a cat on the way to the reception and superglued it to his head. His glasses were held on with a huge rubber band.

I said to the photographer, "I don't care how many photos you get of Barry and me, just make sure you get plenty of the trumpet player!"

Barry and I were so busy talking to people, we didn't have time to eat, so the caterer said he would make a basket for us to take to the hotel. As we got ready to leave, we asked him for it. He sheepishly told us that someone had set fire to our basket and our supper had burned! And all the rest of the food was gone. (I love this stuff!!)

One more hitch. The limo driver had gotten drunk and left.

Barry and I stood in our "going away" outfits, waving good-bye to everyone at the reception and wondering what to do next. Then William rose to the occasion. "I'll drive you!"

We all laughed the whole way to our honeymoon suite. (God has such a cool sense of humor.)

The next morning I asked Barry about the limousine. "Didn't it seem a little strange to you? I mean, the driver looked at me like he was giving me his condolences."

Barry laughed. "My dad got a bargain."

"What do you mean, he got a bargain?"
"He got the limo from his friend at Stuhr's Funeral Home!"
We laughed till we cried.

. . . .

—Unexpected Grace

It's a Man Thang!

● ● ● Thelma Wells

Sometimes a husband feels that if a woman is in the house, he should not have to do much. It's a man thang! And it's hard teaching an old dog new tricks. In our family, we had to accept that Daddy's job was to keep up the cars and the lawn equipment, fix stuff around the house, and supervise. Asking him to do any housework was, well, ineffective. Some things you just can't change. But the truth is, he was helping a lot because seldom did we get into a dirty car or run out of gas for the lawn mower or have to hire a handyman. We really couldn't complain. Most of the time, everything worked out all right. Each of us played a part and appreciated the others' contributions

So, Baby, be proactive. Rather than being passive, manipulative, or angry, work on communicating clearly with your family members. Be forthright about what you want and need, and be willing to listen and negotiate about what each person can contribute to the smooth running of the household. Things can change. Get started.

. . . .

—*Girl, Have I Got Good News for You*

Daddy Goes with Me

● ● ● Luci Swindoll

*W*hen I was about ten, I decided to run away from home. I'd been planning it in my little brain for about a week and had taken a small suitcase off the closet shelf, opened it on my bed, and began packing—a few clothes, a few books, a few toys, and my favorite scrapbook from Momo, my grandmother. As I was making progress, my dad walked by the door, saw what I was doing, and came in. He sat on the end of the bed.

"What's up?" he asked.

"I'm leaving, Daddy. I don't want to live here anymore."

"Okay," he said, very calmly looking at my suitcase. "But what happened to make you want to do this?" He was genuinely concerned . . . ever so sweet and eager to know what had upset me.

"I never get to do anything my way. I don't like the food here. I'm sick of always having to mind. There are too many rules. It's a bunch of stuff . . . so I'm running away!" My voice was cracking.

"Where will you eat, honey?" he asked. "Who will love you when you're sick? What will you do when you run out of money?"

I reminded him I had my two-dollar allowance.

"Two dollars won't go very far," he said. "But if you're determined to go, I'll help you pack. In fact, I'll go with you."

Well. That was worse! *Daddy wants me to go,* I thought, *or he wouldn't offer to help.* It was a very confusing moment. I was stuck in a dilemma and needed something to change, but I didn't know what. I just wanted relief from my childish predicament and thought running away would do it.

After talking with my dad for a while, though, and having him pay such thoughtful attention to my heart with his heart, I felt better and finally settled down and unpacked.

My father had no idea what wisdom he showed at that moment, but it affected me for life. His love entrusted me with a sense of security. Because he wanted to go with me wherever I went, he modeled what God was like—that He would never leave me. To this day, I can travel unafraid all over the world because my daddy instilled in me assurance by his love and by hearing me out. It was an unforgettable moment.

When we listen with our hearts, it's amazing how the action taken as a result can alter people's lives forever.

. . . .

—*Life! Celebrate It*

Brace for Impact!

● ● ● Barbara Johnson

For many parents, the funniest—and potentially the most terrifying—memories originate during those nail-biter days when our teenagers are learning to drive. Few things are more challenging than sitting in the passenger seat while a brand-new driver confidently assures us, "Relax, Mom. I know what I'm doing."

One mom of two teenagers said she thought her arms had permanently frozen in the "brace position" after spending two consecutive years riding in the passenger seat beside her learner's-permit drivers. During one hair-raising episode, she said, they were riding down a two-lane highway on the outskirts of town. Her fifteen-year-old son, who had gotten his permit the week before, was at the wheel, and his fourteen-year-old sister was in the backseat.

"I knew there was a produce stand up ahead, so I gave Marcus plenty of warning that I wanted to stop there," she recalled. "Several cars were coming toward us in the other lane, and Marcus apparently didn't want to have to wait for them to pass before he could turn, so he abruptly swung the steering wheel to the left, barely missing the oncoming traffic. When I opened my eyes, we were sailing down the left-side shoulder with cars whizzing by us on our right and a train rolling beside us on the tracks to our left. It all made me dizzy, and I just kept screaming and closed my eyes again."

The produce stand—and a light pole—were still about a quarter-mile ahead. And while Marcus's two terrified passengers braced for impact, Marcus calmly cruised full-speed down the left-hand shoulder, missing the light pole by inches. Finally he skidded to a stop right in front of the tomato bin, enveloping the business and its customers in a storm cloud of dust and gravel. It was, said the mom, one of the most spectacular arrivals ever made at that quiet little countryside business.

Whether you're gliding smoothly through this segment of the motherhood highway—or screaming your lungs out in the passenger seat—I hope that somehow you'll find a way to have fun and enjoy the ride. Someday, if your mind is still intact when the dust settles, you can look back on this challenging time and cherish the memories you've shared with your kids during their adolescent and teenage years.

. . . .

—*Humor Me, I'm Your Mother*

"Looks like another case of PTKD paralysis—
Parent Teaching Kid to Drive."

©2007 Barbara Johnson

God's Heart for His Girls

● ● ●   Jan Silvious

When I was a little girl, I hated to put on the tight little cotton socks that were part of a four-year-old girl's wardrobe in those days. My daddy knew I hated the pulling and the tugging. I often dawdled when I should have been dressing myself, so mornings were a hassle for me and my parents. I just didn't like those socks.

I remember the relief I felt one morning when I came half awake and realized that my daddy was putting my socks on for me. His help made it so much easier for me to face the day. I didn't have to do what I hated!

At the time, I was a little girl with a little girl's perspective on socks. I didn't like them, and there was nothing in me that was going to come around to seeing the necessity of struggling to put those socks on. Knowing my struggle and my little-girl immaturity, my daddy had compassion on me. He came in my room and put my socks on my sleepy little feet every morning for months before he left for work.

When I was old enough to handle the sock situation, though, he stopped helping me out. I could put on my own socks, and so I did. To continue helping me would have crippled my maturity. I needed to grow, to become stronger, more mature and more responsible. He stepped aside, to my advantage.

God has the same heart toward His girls. His plan for us

is that we will grow up, not just from little girls to big girls, but from Little Girls to Big Girls who can step into all He desires us to be. Throughout the process He is always with us, gently nudging us with compassion and help until we can "get it" for ourselves.

If you really knew what God had in mind for you before you were born, you would be blown away. . . .

God loves us beyond knowing. That is sometimes hard to believe, because we can't see God in the flesh, but every word of this passage is true. Three years ago, I went with my pregnant daughter-in-law to get a 3-D baby scan. She had been through the usual sonograms, but none of them showed us the baby's face. This time, we hoped for a clearer view of her firstborn. The room was dark and the monitor was hazy as the technician rolled the scanning bar across her belly. Then we saw it: Baby Rachel's face appeared on the screen. Her eyes, her nose, her little chubby cheeks, and even her hair standing straight up! How amazed we were. Before Rachel left her mommy's womb, we knew her.

When Rachel was born, we recognized her because we had seen her before. There she was, uniquely herself with her hair standing straight up! When her daddy laid her in my arms, I recognized the face that had been knit together deep in her mama's belly. I was thrilled finally to know this amazing little baby, whom I had seen even before she had come into the light of day. That early glimpse took my breath away and only made me love her more when I first held her. Later I thought, *If I can feel that surge of incredible joy over the birth of one of my little granddaughters, how much greater is the Father-heart of God toward His girls?*

Just imagine how heaven grew silent and His heart must have swelled with joy when—"Whaaaaaaaa!"—you had arrived on earth to become, to be, to live! Another baby girl, created by Him, was born! God is crazy about you! From the moment of your conception, He hovered over every week of your growth in the womb as you came to resemble more and more the person He designed you to be. He watched intently as you made your way into the world, screaming, writhing, and adjusting to earth's air. His complex little girl had been launched on her journey, which already was recorded in His book.

He knew your beginning.

He knew the family that would shape you.

And yes, He even knew the struggles you would have along the way.

He knew them then and He knows them now. You can say without doubt,

How precious are your thoughts about me, O God!
    They are innumerable!
I can't even count them;
    they outnumber the grains of sand!
And when I wake up in the morning,
    you are still with me! (Psalm 139:17–18 NLT)

He doesn't leave you during the night. He doesn't get busy and forget you are here facing challenges. He is with you! . . .

No matter how long your journey has been so far, He has been beside you every step of the way, hovering, listening, standing back and watching, and waiting. Perhaps He has even shed tears for you, His complex little creation, because He, like any good father, will never overpower your will. He launches you. He watches you. He loves you.

. . . .

—*Big Girls Don't Whine*

Don't Be Mad, Okay?

● ● ●　Lowell Streiker

*L*ate one Saturday evening I was awakened by the ringing of my phone. In a sleepy, grumpy voice, I said, "Hello."

The party on the other end of the line paused for a moment before rushing breathlessly into a lengthy speech. "Mom, this is Susanna and I'm sorry I woke you up, but I had to call because I'm going to be a little late getting home. See, Dad's car has a flat, but it's not my fault. Honest! I don't know what happened. The tire just went flat while we were inside the theater. Please don't be mad, okay?"

Since I don't have any daughters, I knew the person had misdialed. "I'm sorry, dear," I replied, "but I have to tell you you've reached the wrong number. I don't have a daughter named Susanna. In fact, I don't have any daughter at all."

A pause. "Gosh, Mom," came the young woman's quavering voice, "I didn't think you'd be this mad.'"

—*Nelson's Big Book of Laughter*

Yahoo!

● ● ● Sheila Walsh

Praise be to the God and Father of our Lord Jesus
Christ! In his great mercy he has given us new birth
into a living hope through the resurrection of Jesus
Christ from the dead, and into an inheritance that
can never perish, spoil or fade—kept in heaven for
you, who through faith are shielded by God's power
until the coming of the salvation that is ready to
be revealed in the last time.
1 Peter 1.3–5

"Dad said I could do it," my son proclaimed as the
sun kissed his blond, sand-filled hair.

"I'm sure Dad was kidding," I replied.

"He wasn't kidding. He's paying for it now," Christian said,
pointing to a small kiosk on the boardwalk.

I looked up and saw Barry walking back to where we sat
on the beach. In his hands he had two life vests.

"Are you nuts?" I inquired as soon as he was within hearing range.

"This will be fun," he said. "The guy said that kids as young
as four can do it."

"That must be families with many, many kids and sun-
stroke," I suggested.

Ignoring my unlikely scenario, Barry and Christian suited
up in their life vests and headed off to the ocean's edge. I

followed right behind. The jet ski instructor began to give them a basic first lesson.

"What if they fall off?" I interrupted.

"That's what the life vests are for," he replied, continuing with his little speech.

"What about sharks?" I continued.

"We don't have sharks here," he said.

"What about jellyfish or big eels—or what about hurricanes that blow up out of nowhere consuming unsuspecting tourists?"

He didn't even answer that one.

"Just one more question," I begged. "Just tell me what the worst is that could happen."

He looked at Barry with great sympathy. "The worst that could happen is that they fall off and float in the water for a few moments. I think they could handle that, don't you?"

I watched as my husband and six-year-old child climbed on a jet ski together and took off across the waves. The faint sound of *yahoos!* floated back to me. Christian told me later that night as he sat in his bath that he had been afraid at first, but he'd so wanted to try it.

"I decided just to go for it, Mom," he said with all the conviction of a true knight.

Once he was fast asleep, I thought about our day and the different ways that my son and I had handled our fear. His fear became a wind behind his back; mine, a pin in the balloon of possibility.

I may never be a jet skier, but I learned a valuable lesson that day. As we face each new day in our journey with Christ, all sorts of things could happen; they might never happen, but they are possibilities. We could have a smooth-as-glass ride. Or severe winds could threaten our craft with the ring of the telephone or the simple act of opening a letter. Waves of circumstance could appear all-consuming.

So what do we know for sure?

Peter reminds us that because of God's great mercy we have a new reality. We are reborn into "a living hope" because of Christ's death and resurrection. We have an inheritance that can never perish, spoil, or fade—kept in heaven for us. It doesn't get any safer than that! Through faith we are shielded by God's power until the end of the age.

We need to hold on to the truth of God's Word every day, for it will be an anchor in a storm and a life vest if we do end up in the water for a while. When we face the worst that could happen in our voyage, we can enjoy the ride, because our hope is a living hope.

I asked Christian about the *yahoos!* the next day

"I guess that's when you were having the most fun," I said.

"No, Mom, that's when I was afraid. I just yelled it anyway."

As you set sail today, the sea may be smooth as glass. If the wind kicks up, however, just lift your head and your heart to heaven and yell a faith-filled *yahoo!*

. . . .

—*Irrepressible Hope*

God (and Uncle Bob) Bring Christmas

● ● ● Mary Graham

> Do not worry about your life.
> —Matthew 6:25

*I*t was Christmas morning, and there wasn't a single gift in the house. When my three brothers and I awakened, there was nothing reflecting the season except a slightly dying, sparsely decorated little tree that Mrs. Cronk, the fifth grade schoolteacher, had given us when school got out for the holidays. The living room was so small that even that little scrawny tree, as pitiful as it was, seemed like an intruder.

"Joy to the World" was being sung on the radio that morning, but there wasn't much joy in the air at our house. Were we sad? Disappointed? Not really. Angry or resentful of our circumstances? Not that I remember. We were the four children (three older brothers and me) still at home with my parents after our three oldest sisters had married and were living several states away. We were poor, but I can't honestly remember if I didn't realize it or if it didn't matter. At any rate, it wasn't an issue. If I had to describe what I felt, that's kind of hard because there was no one to blame or be mad at. It was just quiet. I think that's what surprised me most. There was no sound—nobody knew quite what to say, and that's what made it so odd. Nothing was ever quiet around our house, but that Christmas you could have heard a pin drop.

My mother was a saint, and the older I get the more I'm aware of the magic she wove into life. She was never complaining or criticizing; never one to compare our circumstances with those of friends or family members; never less than grateful that God had given us, as it says in I Timothy 6:17, "richly all things to enjoy" (NKJV). Maybe she was brainwashing us, but for some reason, whatever the circumstances, they never seemed to bother her; so, consequently, they didn't bother us.

She gave of herself in amazing ways. And she gave not only to us, but seemingly to everyone. The less she had, the more she gave, and the happier she seemed. Jesus Himself taught that it's more blessed to give than to receive. I never really doubted that, since I'd seen the genuine demonstration of that truth in the life of my mother. God had given her a job to do, and she did it with a happy heart. If I ever thought about complaining, she'd say convincingly, "Oh, honey, don't think about that now."

Times have changed since the early 1950s when my mother couldn't quite make ends meet. But I'm always reminded that she could put joy in the hearts of her children just by being there for us with a spirit of thanksgiving and joy. She didn't try to be something she wasn't or buy stuff she couldn't. She called upon her Savior to give peace and assurance that He would meet our needs. She was an amazing woman of faith. She encouraged us by her presence and calm. One of the hardest things I've ever tried to do is be objective about my mother. That, to me, would be like being objective about Mother Teresa.

Here's what happened that Christmas. About midday, my

uncle Bob—an attorney in a nearby town—showed up unexpectedly with his family. They brought turkey, ham, all the trimmings, and their little sedan full of presents for all. They walked in, announcing that it was boring and lonely at their house (which was, incidentally, huge, warm, brand new, and decorated beautifully for the holidays). They wanted to be with us. And did we ever want to be with them! Many years earlier when my parents were newlyweds, Mother had taken this little brother of hers under her wing. She provided nurture and care and somehow was able to help him through law school. He adored my parents, and the feeling was mutual.

God made a way for Uncle Bob through my parents, and now God was making a way for us through him. God can do anything! And in the process He demonstrated great faithfulness to a little girl who, fifty years later, has not forgotten.

....

—Contagious Joy

A Little Too Much Time on the Road

● ● ● Sandi Patty

nna's history includes a funny story about her nursery-school days. One day when the class was going to make pancakes, the teacher went around the room asking the students what ingredients they would use. As her classmates answered confidently, "flour," "sugar," "eggs," Anna got increasingly irritated. Finally she raised her hand and said, "No, this is how you make pancakes: you get them out of the freezer, put them on a plate, cook them in the microwave, put syrup on them, and eat them." Then she added emphatically, "*That's how you make pancakes.*"

When her teacher told me that story I thought, *Hmmmm. Maybe we've spent a little too much time on the road living in an RV!*

. . . .

—*Life in the Blender*

A Sweet Reprieve from Cucumbers

● ● ● Chonda Pierce

Our favorite thing to do on Easter Sunday was to see what the rich kids were wearing 'cause we knew that's what we'd be wearing the next Easter.

Along with Scripture verses, choruses, manners, and the proper dress code, the greatest thing my mother passed on to us was the gift of adaptation. I am almost certain that my mother invented the phrase "When life gives you lemons . . ." Mom and Dad instilled in us not only the joy of a good glass of lemonade but also the thrill of making it yourself!

We never considered ourselves well-off financially. We seldom considered ourselves poor. We simply didn't consider *ourselves*. My wardrobe was filled with hand-me-downs and homemade dresses my grandmother would send us every fall for the upcoming school year. When we wore shoes, they were usually tennis shoes or sandals. Since we lived in the South, barefoot was vogue!

There did come a brief time when the realization that "We *are* poor" hit us all. Mother couldn't find a job. Dad had just accepted a call to a small church in Orangeburg, South Carolina. Mike had gone to a college five hundred miles away, and Charlotta was soon to follow. I can remember hearing Mom and Dad argue about the possibility of getting food stamps. I don't think it was as much a matter of pride as it was that Mom still didn't consider us desperate enough. She would say, "But what if someone else needs them more?"

As I sat at the dinner table eating for the fifth time that week a sandwich made with government cheese and grilled with government butter, I looked at her and said, "Mom, who could need 'em worse than us?"

So one afternoon Mom and I stood in the food stamp line for more than three hours. Of course, after we got them, the whole family wanted in on the selection process at the grocery store. Grocery shopping had never been so exciting. Everyone was thrilled to pick out the food, but as soon as we approached the checkout counter, they all scrambled to the car—except for Mom and me. When Mother handed the girl at the Piggly Wiggly our little booklet, I grinned at Mother and said in my most Southern-belle, Scarlet O'Hara voice, "I'll tell the driver to bring the limo around, Mother, and pick us up at the door. I know how you hate to wait in this summer heat." When the food stamps ran out, we went back to grilled cheese until things began to pick up at the church again.

Mother had toyed a long time with the idea of going to nursing school. When she heard that Baptist Hospital in Columbia, South Carolina, was offering a two-year Licensed Practical Nurse (LPN) course, she decided that this would be the year. She and Dad argued about her decision for hours— but for some reason, Mother truly felt nursing school was something she was called to do. She borrowed the money from her mother, and at the age of forty off to school she went.

She drove ninety-one miles round trip to nursing school every day. Cheralyn and I made flashcards and quizzed her for exams. She amazed us all. Mother had not been in school in twenty-two years and would have failed chemistry in high school twice had it not been for the tutor her mom and dad had hired during her senior year. She passed nursing school with flying colors, and we proudly attended her graduation from LPN school. (Dad had refused to attend—but near the end of the ceremony we noticed him on the back row of that huge auditorium in Columbia.)

While Mom was in nursing school, Cheralyn and I had almost full responsibility of the house. We had our regular chores to do as well as cooking most of the meals. We were proud of our diverse menus: macaroni and cheese, peanut butter and jelly, Froot Loops—and on special occasions (or Friday, whichever came first), *hot dogs*!

Did I mention that we lived on a tight budget? We had a few poundings from the church folks—but you get mostly dusty, dented cans of yams and cranberry sauce at those things! So Cheralyn and I decided the answer to our menu problem was simply to grow our own garden. We worked for hours getting the soil ready. We saved our money and went down to the local hardware store and purchased seed packets of green beans, corn, cucumbers, and tomatoes. The weeds outgrew our patience, and our sandy southern soil could produce nothing—nothing but cucumbers, that is.

They were everywhere! We had a long vine of cucumbers that stretched from the front porch of our house, across the church parking lot, and up the steps of the fellowship hall. We made cucumber sandwiches, cucumber salad, fried cucumbers—anything you could make with cucumbers, we made. Some things you couldn't make with cucumbers we made anyway. And we ate them all.

Then just like the plagues finally ended in Egypt, we

received a sweet reprieve from our cucumber suppers. A man in our church raised hogs for his chain of barbecue restaurants. He called the house one evening to say that the next morning he would be stopping by with a package for the pastor and his family. Hallelujah!

Cheralyn and I rewrote our menu for the next month: barbecued pork chops, ribs, ham, bacon—we even made plans for the ears and the feet. We set the table that night for tomorrow's dinner. We were so excited we could hardly sleep. (Or maybe it was the cucumbers!)

Nevertheless, as promised, an old pickup truck pulled into the driveway the next afternoon. A kind old farmer climbed out of his truck carrying a huge package wrapped in brown paper. The front of his apron was bloody, but we hardly pitied the beast we would dine on for the next few weeks. We could smell something spicy and delicious as he set the package on the counter. We had envisioned a huge country ham, perhaps a pork roast, maybe slabs of bacon. We couldn't wait for him to leave so we could dive in.

Mother thanked him very kindly, and as the front door clicked shut, Cheralyn and I ripped open our mouth-watering feast. There it was—a fresh, meaty, fifteen-pound roll of *bologna*! Now don't get me wrong. I don't dislike bologna. But a couple of skinny little preacher's kids had waited all day long for pork chops and had gotten bologna—disappointing bologna.

When Mother fixed supper that night, we were surprised to see something shaped like pork chops on our plates. Mother had used some of her arts and crafts skills to cut little pork chop shapes out of the bologna and fried it until it was crisp. Served with cold, sliced cucumbers and cornbread, Mom showed us how to make lemonade out of lemons.

The next day the doorbell rang. A young lady stood on our

porch and explained to Mother how she had noticed the church next door and wondered if we knew how to reach the pastor. Mother invited her in. With watery eyes, she told Mother that her children were hungry and that her husband had been out of work for several months. Her food stamps had run out too. Without question, Mom quickly filled a grocery sack with cucumbers and cut our much-needed roll of bologna in half and shared it with this stranger. They shared a glass of lemonade before she left, and we never saw her again.

Be kind and compassionate to one another, forgiving each other, just as in Christ God forgave you. (Ephesians 4:32)

. . . .

—Second Row, Piano Side

Baby Doll

● ● ● Patsy Clairmont

I was almost nine and a half when my mom gave me a long, gift-wrapped box for Christmas. I quickly pulled the paper off the present and lifted the lid in anticipation. It was just as I had suspected and exactly what I wanted: a doll. When given the opportunity, I was a feisty linebacker in our neighborhood and could tackle with the best of them, yet I loved my dolls. I owned several, and a couple of them were my dear friends: Toni, a brunette whom you could give home permanents; and Dydee, a lovable baby doll who blew bubbles and wet her diaper. Dydee was, as the kids say today, way cool.

The new arrival was a show-stopper, a red-haired bride doll touting a pearl necklace and bracelet. Mom told me all the doll's clothes had been hand designed, including her hoop slip and lacy garter. Mom emphasized that the doll was very special. Have you noticed that "special" is often a setup for moms to lower the boom? Mom then announced that this was to be my last doll because, in her words, I was now too old.

Too old? Too old? Why, I was still wearing undershirts and Mary Janes with lacy anklets and consuming Baby Huey comic books. Suddenly I didn't like this red-haired whippet of a doll, this intruder, this gown-clad demarcation between childhood and a job at the dime store. I was not ready for a last doll.

I still own that doll, and as the years have stockpiled into half a century, she has remained in her box waiting for a playmate. Fat chance. At some point she must have been in a damp environment because during a move I lifted her lid, and she looked a bit jaundiced, and her red wig had detached from her head and had slid sideways. She looked loopy. I sneered. Too old my foot!

Oh, I forgave Mom. Honest. But not totally until I was thirteen. That was when Mom presented me with a sister, Elizabeth Ann. She was even better than Dydee because all her orifices worked, and like Toni, you could fix baby Beth's thick hair in all sorts of outrageous styles. I had been the "only" child for four years—since Don had joined the army— and I was ready for company, especially in the form of a *real* baby doll.

— *I Grew Up Little*

I Know Where I'm Going

● ● ● Sheila Walsh

"Do you know what my favorite two things about you are, Mom?" Christian asked me one day.

"I don't think I do," I said. "Is it my cooking?"

"No, but I do love your penne pasta."

"Is it my jokes?" I asked.

"Definitely not!" he said.

"Well, what then?" I asked, my feelings slightly wounded from the joke thing.

"I love that you love me, and I love your personality," he said.

"That is so sweet, Christian, thank you. What do you like about my personality?"

"I like that you love your life, Mom, and I get to be in it."

I thought about that for a while. My son's comments touched me deeply. I knew, too, that they had not always been true. For many years, I just got through my life. It's really only in the last ten or twelve years that I have loved it, and I have felt so grateful to be alive.

Like Dorothy and her friends as they traveled to the Emerald City, I have been changed by the journey. What once would have terrified me no longer holds that power. It's not that I have become a stronger person, but I know where I am going, and I know who is with me. I know that at every twist and turn of the road, Christ will be there, and because of that fact alone, I am not afraid.

We are all on a journey in this life; we have no choice on that front, but we are either growing or shrinking inside. We are either becoming more fully the woman that God knows us to be or becoming less recognizable daily. Like Eve, we will one day be given the gift of beholding Jesus face-to-face and eating freely from the tree of life, but what about now? The tree is guarded until then, but Jesus has promised living water to sustain us until that day.

. . . .

—*I'm Not Wonder Woman, But God Made Me Wonderful!*

Mama T's Light-Bulb Moment

● ● ● Thelma Wells

*M*y granny didn't cut corners, and neither do I. Honey, I cut so there's hardly anything left *but* the corner! You see, I travel nearly thirty weekends a year with Women of Faith, and I run two ministries and write books and do all sorts of other things. So if there's a quick-and-easy way to do something, that's the Mama T way.

For starters, let me tell you the key word in hosting an informal get-together: *plastic*. Back in the old days, before I got smart, I refused to allow anything plastic in my house. That's right. Paper plates were for picnics, and I don't like flies and ants, so I don't do picnics! I used my fine china and crystal every time I had company. And let me tell you, I have some nice stuff. I loved sitting at the dining room table with my guests (before it became the eating place of last resort) and looking out over all the brightly polished gold flatware, the twinkling crystal glasses, the gleaming china plates and serving pieces, the sparkling chafing dishes, and the perfectly pressed cloth napkins. But as time went on, making sure all that stuff was polished and twinkling and gleaming and sparkling and pressed got to be a real drag, and I ain't kiddin'! I was working myself silly, and I even started dreading these get-togethers instead of delighting in them. In short, as my family grew with the addition of in-laws and grandkids—I grew tired!

Plus, I didn't want my grandkids to come to my house and hear me telling them all the time, "Don't touch that!" "Don't drop that!" "Be careful!" When our children were small, we had a relative like that, and whenever we went to her house, she spent the whole time fussing at the kids, worried they would break her stuff. And you know what? The only place we went where my kids ever broke things was her house. We were all so nervous and on edge around her, it just seemed inevitable.

So one Sunday, after everyone had left and I was still in the kitchen washing and drying and putting away all the china and crystal and silver, I gave myself a good talkin' to. I said, "Thelma, you got up at 5 a.m. in Pittsburgh, flew several hundred miles, went to church, put on a feast for your family, and now it's nearly 9 p.m. and you're still in the kitchen. What are you thinkin', girl? You're runnin' yourself into the ground—and you're way too smart for that. Get yourself some plastic plates and flatware and cups and napkins and a big ol' trash can, and next time you put on a feed for your family, you use that stuff and you just *see* if the world comes to an end."

Well, guess what. That's what I did. And although it bothered me a little at first, it didn't seem to bother anyone else—especially the women who helped with the cleanup. So now for our Sunday gatherings, I use plastic and paper everything: cups, plates, flatware, napkins. Even the punch bowl is plastic. (But that's my secret; everyone who looks at it thinks it's crystal.) I use it because it's the perfect size for mixing my secret-recipe fruit tea (sorry, honey, that's one recipe I just don't share), and we ladle it right out of that fancy-looking plastic punch bowl with a fancy-looking plastic ladle into ordinary plastic cups. And so far, no one has suffered death by plasticide. So girlfriend, if you want to get me a present, don't send me a crystal bowl or fancy serving plate or a set of linen napkins. You just send me some plastic!

··

—*Listen Up, Honey*

Baby, It's Cold Inside!

● ● ● Patsy Clairmont

I just came in from doing three jumping jacks, four knee bends, and jogging around the mailbox twice. Nope, I'm not on a new exercise program; I just needed to warm up. Not for a marathon, I assure you.

See, Les has a habit of cranking our house thermostat down to the chill factor of Antarctica, so I periodically have to de-ice my bones. I've become accustomed to the frost dangling off my eyebrows, but the icicles in my sandals still annoy me. I think it's those pointy ends. Here's the bottom line: when one must wear flannel PJs and thick socks to bed in July (hello, July!), something's amiss with wedded bliss.

Les and I just celebrated forty-three years of marriage, so I know I should be used to how differently we are calibrated. But when I have to leave the house just to thaw out, it rankles me a tad. In addition to maintaining a year-round winter freeze, Les has a need to crunch ice, a glassful at a time. Of course, I have a need to gripe about his crunching ice, a glassful at a time. Isn't it great how we meet each other's needs?

—All Cracked Up

Does This Thing Come with Directions?

● ● ● Sheila Walsh

For his fortieth birthday, some friends gave my husband, Barry, a garden hammock. It came in five separate boxes and required some assembly. I am an assembly geek, so I told him that if he unpacked it, I would assemble it. Unfortunately, Barry threw the instructions away with the rest of the trash, and I was left in the yard knee-deep in parts. My eight-year-old son, Christian, said that he would help. We tried for two hours to find which bits connected to other bits but to no avail. I sat on the grass, totally frustrated, when Barry called out enthusiastically, "All I can remember is that it said it was easy to assemble!"

....

I'm Not Wonder Woman, But God Made Me Wonderful!

"I need a card that says, 'Sorry I used your
new bathrobe to wax the car.'"

©2004 John McPherson. Used by permission of John McPherson. Included in the book Close to Home Revisited.

Big-Girl Talk

● ● ● Jan Silvious

I remember a night in my late twenties when a discussion about a toothbrush brought about a life-altering change in my maturity.

Charlie, my husband, had spent the better part of the day cleaning the shower in our bathroom. When it was time to go to bed, I could not find my toothbrush, and so I asked him if he knew where it was. He, of course, denied any knowledge of my toothbrush. Well, he may not have known anything about it, but I knew it had been there in the morning, and I knew that between then and bedtime, he had used a brush to clean the shower. Instead of being grateful that the shower had been meticulously cleaned, and instead of applying the wisdom of abandoning the quarrel before it begins (see Proverbs 17:14), I chose to make my point. Relentlessly.

I became a virtual Perry Mason. "Well, if you didn't take my toothbrush, then who did? You used a brush. Where did you get it? If you didn't use my toothbrush, then whose brush did you use?" By the time my inquisition reached fever pitch, Charlie got out of bed, pulled his pants on, threw on a shirt, and walked out the front door without a word. That made me mad, but I thought, *Good, he's gone.*

Then I heard the tearful voice of a little boy crying in the next room. I had no idea that one of our sons was awake and had heard the whole exchange. Not only had he listened to

147

his Little-Girl mother natter on about her toothbrush, he heard his daddy leave abruptly in what was for this young child the middle of the night. His little mind had to be confused and hurting. He was trying to figure out what on earth was going on in his family. I went to his room to try to comfort him. He was crying in his pillow, sobbing, "My daddy is gone and he's not coming back." I assured him that his daddy would be back and that everything was fine; we had just been talking about a toothbrush. (A ridiculous explanation, but the best I had to offer.) He quieted down, and I went back to our room to seethe until Charlie returned.

I soon heard his key in the lock and his footsteps on the stairs.

He came into our room, tossed six new toothbrushes on the bed, and calmly said, "Brush your teeth and let's go to bed." Well, I brushed my teeth and I went to bed, but I couldn't sleep for thinking about the little boy, my precious son, who had been profoundly affected by his mother's Little-Girl stand. Right or wrong, I had made a choice that had wounded the youngest, most vulnerable member of our family.

That incident marked the beginning of significant growth for me. Being faced with the stark reality about yourself is often the first step toward growing up and wanting to leave behind your childish ways. In fact, I would say, it is the best and only way to learn. When you see yourself for who you are and for what you are doing, the choice to change becomes evident. I had to face the reality that I would have to put away my childish speaking, or people I loved were going to be profoundly, permanently affected.

Now, it took me a while to understand that the choice to change was mine, but the actual changing was something that God would have to do in me. He allows life circumstances to do the convincing, and then He lovingly, graciously comes along and does for us and in us what we cannot do for ourselves. I could want to change; I could decide to change; I could modify my behavior, but God had to accomplish the permanent change that I could depend on. I could put away the thing I didn't like to do; but God is the one who could lock the cupboard door.

I have since come to love 1 Corinthians 13:11, which says, "When I was a child, I spoke and thought and reasoned as a child does. But when I grew up, I put away childish things" (NLT). I realize this verse appears in the context of spiritual gifts, but truth is truth no matter the context. If doing away with childish things is relevant to spiritual gifts, surely it is relevant to life as well.

—*Big Girls Don't Whine*

If It's Important, Write It Down!

● ● ● Sandi Patty

I insist that all our activities and everything we're doing must be recorded on a "written" calendar. I have a bulletin board and a dry-erase marker board in the kitchen—I call it Grand Central. Everyone's supposed to leave me notes there, either tacked to the cork board or written on the marker board. Then I add their events to the calendar I keep on my computer, where it's easily updated. I print out a new copy of the month's activities every time something is added and post it on Grand Central. Occasionally, when we have a lot going on, I distribute copies to those I call the "heads of state": all the parents and grandparents and other adults who help us stay on track.

At least that's how it's supposed to work. Recently I called a family meeting to announce that I was tired of being told at the last minute that someone had an event that night and we all needed to be there. I didn't want to get any more calls while I was out on the road from someone who had forgotten to tell me about an appointment or a meeting or something that required a parent's signature.

"That stuff drives me crazy," I said. "So remember: if there is something important I should know about, *put it in writing* and stick it to that bulletin board in the kitchen. If you think of something and realize, *I need to remind Mom about that*, write it on the marker board. Is that clear? Does everyone understand? I will look at Grand Central and expect to find anything important you want me to know. Then I'll put it on the calendar and make sure you have a ride or a signature, or I'll be there to cheer for you if you're in some kind of event. But you've gotta give me some advance warning. Got it? IF IT'S SOMETHING I NEED TO KNOW, PUT IT IN WRITING!" . . .

Later that night, when the house was quiet, I happened to walk by Grand Central and see a tiny piece of paper folded into a square and tacked up in the corner. On the outside of it, someone had written, "Mom."

When I unfolded it, this is what I read.

Mom, I love you.
Sam

That's what he thought I needed to know.

Okay, now, just let me . . . get a tissue . . . and dab my eyes a minute. (And they say my family meetings are worthless? That little note alone is priceless proof that they're worth every raucous minute of the chaos they generate.)

. . . .

—Life in the Blender

Part 5

Healthy Hilarity

Laughing Is Merry Medicine

• • • • •

Let me tell you, the more the pleasures of the
body fade away, the greater to me is the
pleasure and charm of conversation.

Plato

Regarding Food . . .

● ● ● Cathy Lee Phillips

*I*n short, everything that tastes good is bad for you. You can eat asparagus and cardboard. All other food raises your cholesterol, your triglycerides, hardens your arteries, causes cancer, hemorrhoids, and adds pounds.

So why are there Krispy Kreme doughnut stores that display the "Hot Doughnuts Now" sign? Why does Mick's Restaurant in Atlanta serve the best Oreo Cheesecake on the planet? And The Varsity the best onion rings? Why does Cracker Barrel offer fluffy biscuits with butter and jam?

I wish I knew the answer to these and many other baffling questions.

I only know that there had better be cheesecake in heaven because that is probably the next time I will get any.

The Butcher's Scales

● ● ● Sheila Walsh

My friend Moira and I gazed at the pictures of the models in our new magazine. A school friend had brought it back from a trip to America, and we were fascinated. Toward the end of the magazine, there was a chart that gave the correct weight range for every height. I had no idea that such a thing existed.

"How tall are you, Moira?" I asked.

"Five feet, two and a bit inches," she said.

"Okay, well you should weigh between one hundred and one hundred and twenty pounds if we don't count the wee bit," I said.

"How much is that?" she asked.

In Scotland, we weighed in stones and pounds. (There are fourteen pounds in each stone.) I took out my calculator from my school bag.

"That's between seven stone two pounds and eight stone eight pounds," I said. "That's quite a margin."

"How tall are you?" Moira asked.

"I am five feet, four inches. What do I get to weigh?"

She studied the chart. "You should be between one hundred and twenty pounds and one hundred and thirty-five pounds. That's between 8:8 and 9:9. What do you weigh?" she asked me.

"I have no idea. What about you?"

"Me either," she said. "We don't have scales at home. Where do you think we could find some?"

"I know!" I said. "Let's ask the butcher—he has to weigh cows, he must be able to handle us."

The butcher was very accommodating and let us slip into the back of his shop and weigh ourselves. Moira discovered that she was just where she should have been at 109 pounds. I, on the other hand, weighed in at 142.

"Good grief!" I said. "I'm half a cow!"

· ·

—*I'm Not Wonder Woman, But God Made Me Wonderful!*

Fat Farm Failures

● ● ● Barbara Johnson

You have a heart of gold.
That would explain why you weigh
two hundred pounds!

*A*fter I had a hysterectomy several years ago, my doctor assured me it was just a myth that women automatically put on extra weight after menopause. "There's no reason why you should gain weight if you eat a sensible diet and get sufficient exercise," he said. The problem is . . . eating sensibly has never seemed like much fun to me!

For nearly a year after my surgery, I steadily gained a pound or two every month. My friend Mickey was experiencing the doctor's idea of the "myth" in the same way. So she and I decided we were never going to lose weight on our own; instead, we agreed we would splurge and have ourselves admitted to a fat farm—a spa located some fifty miles north of Los Angeles, out in the desert. Friends warned us we wouldn't get much to eat at this place, so we stopped at a fried chicken restaurant on the way for a bucket of reinforcements. We also took crackers and snacks in our luggage and sneaked everything into our room at the spa.

Sure enough; our friends were right. The food wasn't just scanty—it was almost microscopic! It did have nice names, however, like soufflé of this and fillet of that. They served a lot of weak tea and fancy little cubes of gelatin with fingernail-size portions of whipped cream. One especially memorable dessert was called "tofu supreme."

We would have starved except for the fried chicken and crackers we ate in our room that first day. For dinner that night they served a small wedge of lettuce and a spoonful of fluffy yogurt.

The next day we had veggie burgers. Have you ever had a veggie burger? At this fat farm, a veggie burger was two very THIN oblong crackers with some strands of carrots, a pile of ground-up broccoli, and some bean sprouts smashed between the crackers! As we studied this sorry excuse for a lunch, Mickey and I had fun wondering what McDonald's might name this concoction if it were added to their menu. I thought they might call it the McSprout or the McSproccoli Mickey opted for the Quarter-Ouncer.

But just thinking of McDonald's when our stomachs were so desperate for some real nourishment (that is, something fried and fattening) made us want to make a break for the nearest golden arches (which were at least a half-hour's drive away). So we couldn't play that game for long!

We were all expected to dress up for dinner each night. So there we sat, looking beautiful and starving to death. We were supposed to stay for four days, but the fried chicken only lasted until the first night, and we ran out of crackers and cheese the next afternoon. It was then that we decided to escape that place while we still had enough energy to make the drive home.

On the way back to LA we stopped at that same fried chicken place. Faint with hunger, we staggered up to the window and ordered the REALLY big bucket.

When someone sent me the following menu, it reminded me of those two long days at the fat farm. I don't know where it came from, but I think you'll quickly see why it's guaranteed to make you lose weight:

MONDAY
Breakfast: Weak tea
Lunch: Bouillon cube in $\frac{1}{2}$ cup water
Dinner: 1 pigeon thigh
3 ounces prune juice (to be gargled only)

TUESDAY
Breakfast: Scraped crumbs from burnt toast
Lunch: 1 doughnut hole
Dinner: 2 canary drumsticks

WEDNESDAY
Breakfast: Boiled-out stains of tablecloth
Lunch: Bellybutton from navel orange
Dinner: Bee's knees and mosquito knuckles

THURSDAY
Breakfast: Shredded eggshell skins
Lunch: $\frac{1}{2}$ dozen poppy seeds
Dinner: 3 eyes from Irish potato (diced)

FRIDAY
Breakfast: 2 lobster antennae
Lunch: 1 guppy fin
Dinner: Fillet of soft-shell crab claws

SATURDAY
Breakfast: 4 chopped banana seeds
Lunch: Broiled butterfly liver
Dinner: Jellyfish vertebrae

SUNDAY
Breakfast: Pickled hummingbird tongue
Lunch: Prime ribs of tadpole
Dinner: Tossed paprika salad
Aroma of empty custard pie plate

Note: All meals are to be placed under a microscope while eaten to make them more filling.
—Source Unknown

Obviously, Mickey and I were big failures at abiding by the rules; instead, we decided to leave the fat farm and farm our fat ourselves! We probably shouldn't have gone together, because neither one of us had enough will power, when it came to food, to turn down a single morsel. We reminded each other of the friend Erma Bombeck described when she said it was just her luck to go to a fat farm and share a room with the only person there who had sewn Reese's Pieces into the hem of her jacket.

* *

—Living Somewhere Between Estrogen and Death

Hundred-Dollar Ringworm

● ● ● Marilyn Meberg

Medical research is wonderfully clear about the benefits of laughter for the body. We know laughter relaxes the skeletal frame, lowers blood pressure, releases those little endorphin painkillers, and expands the blood vessels. What is new in medical research is the benefit of laughter for that often ignored but vitally important organ— the liver. Apparently, laughter is the one human activity that exercises the liver. I never knew the liver was in need of exercise, but just knowing laughter does for my liver what laughter does for my blood pressure causes me to dash about for daily humor with the well-being of my liver in mind.

No one has helped exercise my liver more than my friend Luci. When the pain of life bears down, the questions are overwhelming, and the answers come more slowly, laughter is the best medicine.

Our Women of Faith conferences are known for the many extraordinary musical artists who perform with us. We've had fabulous experiences with artists like Stephen Curtis Chapman, Amy Grant, CeCe Winans, Kristen Chenowith, Sandi Patty, Nicole Nordeman, and many others who include Women of Faith in their busy performance schedules. One of my favorite groups is Avalon. They not only do "knock-ya-down-drag-you-around" fantastic musical presentations, but they're warm, fun, and compelling human beings who love Jesus.

During one of their weekends with us, we were sitting in the green room laughing and sharing crazy stories. Many of my most memorable moments are times Luci and I have managed to get one another in a little trouble. When that happens, one of us ends up buying the other one's dinner. That day, the storytelling backstage prompted Jody McBrayer, one of the Avalon soloists, to say to me as we were walking to our seats, "Marilyn, aren't you up to speak next?"

"Yeah."

"Well, I have a great idea, but I'm not going to tell you what it is until we walk out of here and head for the stage."

Of course I was intrigued.

So, as we exited the green room, Jody fell into step with me and said, "I'll give you fifty bucks if you can somehow work the word *ringworm* into your speech."

I hooted.

"Are you kidding, Jody—*ringworm*?"

"Yup! It's worth fifty bucks to me to see if you can somehow weave that word into whatever you say this afternoon. But the deal is, you have to make it seem to fit."

I was hooked. "Okay, Jody. But I'll have to have more than fifty bucks. I'll need one hundred. I mean, really, *ringworm* is worth a hundred."

He thought for a second and said, "Okay, but remember, *ringworm* has to make sense. You can't just shout the word out of the blue."

"You've got a deal, Jody!"

I then took my seat on the porch. With only a few moments for deep-think, I leaned over to Luci and whispered, "Do you mind if I say you have ringworm?"

"What . . . ?"

"Do you mind if I say that you have ringworm?"

She snorted back, "I don't have ringworm . . . never have had ringworm, you birdbrain . . . what are you talking about?"

"Jody will pay me a hundred bucks if I can work the word *ringworm* into my speech. Can I say you have it? I'll take you to lunch with the victory money."

Her eyes brightened, the deal was made, and I went onstage.

Each week toward the end of my speech, I describe a time Luci recently popped by my house with Starbucks. In that time, we caught up on stuff and exercised our livers. As she was exiting my driveway, for some reason she was not backing out in a straight line but was slowly veering into my newly planted petunias. It was at this point in my speech that I decided to change the story line and throw in the word *ringworm*. So I told the audience I hated to correct Luci as she backed into my petunias, because she has periodic outbreaks of ringworm. I worried that maybe her medication was too strong this time. I explained that one of the little-known side effects of ringworm medication is an overwhelming desire to be enveloped by petunias. So actually, I could not really fault her for veering into my petunias—it was a drug-induced response. The audience registered a combination of sympathy, confusion, and disbelief. Luci was beaming in anticipation of a free lunch and seemingly not the slightest bit concerned about her false skin condition or that I had made it a matter of public knowledge.

I had not had time to warn the porch pals, so they were hooting with this unexpected touch of craziness. Luci jumped to her feet as Jody dashed over to hug her. They did a little dance while I explained to the audience that Luci did not really have ringworm. I told them I had just earned a hundred bucks from Jody, who bet me I could not work the word *ringworm* into my speech. Actually, I was the one who felt like doing a victory dance. Once all that was made clear, the audience joined in with enthusiastic cheering and clapping.

So there you have it, dear ones: a little exercise for our livers. Thanks, Jody, from all of us!

. . . .

—Since You Asked

Touchy about Being Touched

● ● ● Barbara Johnson

Maternity clothes are different now. Today many pregnant gals let it all hang out, wearing tiny little T-shirts and low-slung slacks or skirts so they can proudly display their new condition. Modern celebrities happily pose to let their "bump" be photographed by the national press. Such exhibitions would have been outrageous during my pregnancies. Back then, the main idea was to hide the obvious as long as possible. So we moms-to-be wore big, loose tops that, on windy days, made us look like circus tents that had pulled loose from their moorings and were drifting down the sidewalk.

One thing that's probably the same for *all* generations of moms-to-be is our feeling about the "touch factor." Most of us do *not* want strangers—or strange relatives—touching our tummies, whether we hide our protruding shape with enough fabric to rig a sailing ship or choose to wear a revealing bikini in our ninth month. And yet, those hands just keep on reaching out and patting us as though the baby-to-be is a pet Chihuahua. I'll bet fashion designers could make a fortune selling maternity T-shirts imprinted with "Private Property," or "Keep Off!"

. . . .

—*Humor Me, I'm Your Mother*

© 2007 Barbara Johnson

Some moms-to-be get a little touchy
about being touched.

Laugh It Up

●　●　● Martha Bolton

*D*id you know the human body is designed to handle an unlimited number of laughs? None of us were born with a warning, "Do not exceed recommended dosage of laughter in a twenty-four-hour period," tattooed on our forehead. From birth to the moment of our death, we are free to enjoy as much laughter as we want. In fact, look at the longevity of some of the greatest comics of our time: George Burns lived to be one hundred years old. Milton Berle was ninety-three when he passed away, and Lucille Ball was seventy-seven. Red Skelton was eighty-four, and Bob Hope's one hundredth birthday was in May of 2003.

Obviously, a good sense of humor is healthy.

Exercise is healthy, but only to a point. We can sweat to just so many oldies. We can run a limited number of miles before we end up collapsing on the jogging trail. We can only do so many push-ups, sit-ups, or knee-bends before our muscles give out and go on strike. Exercise is good for us, but in moderation.

We can't eat all the red meat we want either. Or butter. Or sugar. Our bodies weren't built to handle an overabundance of any of these products. We can certainly handle some, but we shouldn't pour that five-pound bag of C & H onto our shredded wheat.

But laughter? As far as our vital organs are concerned, there's no limit. Our heart won't start beating irregularly if we have a fit of laughter. We won't dehydrate, our kidneys won't start shutting down, and we won't run the risk of our lungs collapsing during a giggle fest. In fact, the more laughter we have in our lives, the healthier we could become. Laughter is good for us.

It's been said that a hearty laugh burns calories. Laughter is also believed to release endorphins into our system that can change our outlook on life and help prevent depression.

Laughter can have positive effects on our immune system, too. It can even improve our social life, because people are far more attracted to those who laugh than those who whine.

Not only can we laugh as much as we want, we can laugh whenever we want. Laughter isn't seasonal. We can do it in the spring, summer, fall, and winter. Laughter doesn't have a curfew. We can stay up and laugh as late as we want. And we can do it first thing in the morning.

We don't have to worry about laughter putting us in debt either. Laughter's free. Unlike that trip to an amusement park, buying a new car, or going outlet shopping, laughter won't stretch our already stretched-out budget. We can enjoy as much laughter as we want and we'll never go over our credit line or be forced to pay 20 percent interest.

It's perfectly legal to laugh and drive, too. (Although if you're in the car by yourself, people might start to stare.)

And laughter doesn't have an expiration date. No matter how old you are, your sense of humor can be just as good as it was when you were a child. It may need a little dusting off, but it isn't due to expire until you do.

So go on, laugh it up. Give your mind a break from the stresses of life. Laughter will never give you a headache. But it can certainly help heal the one you might already have.

. . . .

—*I Think, Therefore I Have a Headache*

The Year We Had Head Lice

● ● ●   Sandi Patty

*N*ow, just let me say, before I tell you this story, that even before our families blended, as a mother of four children I was quite experienced in the principles of infectious and contagious ailments. After all, I had lived through the ordeal of having a child (eight-year-old Anna) break out with chicken pox in between the first and second halves of a dance recital, probably infecting the whole cast and most of the audience! (But really, I couldn't be concerned about all of them; I soon had my hands full with my own little isolation ward and four little chicken-poxed patients.)

I'm also the mother who, after we had blended, would not hesitate in a physician's office to ask, when a child was diagnosed with strep throat, "Uh, Doctor, would you mind just writing out seven more prescriptions of the antibiotic to save me the extra trips?"

I had weathered all sorts of contagious viruses and infections, and I felt confident I could handle anything else that tried to attack my family. But then the head lice sneaked in. Looking back on it now, Don and I laugh hysterically. But when it happened, we were just plain hysterical.

Let me point out that we were experienced, even in head lice. When the kids were little, we'd had a brief encounter with one or two of the kids. We'd done the treatment, and the lice had disappeared.

Then came the year when the upper grades at the kids' elementary school had a short exchange program with a school overseas, and one of the exchange students stayed briefly with us. Jenn was especially excited about having a friend from overseas, and she offered to share her room with this pleasant young guest student—I'll call her Francine.

All went well for a while, then one morning Jenn came in and whispered, "Mom, Francine's got head lice!"

"How do you know?" I whispered back.

"I just know, Mom! I'm sure of it," Jenn said.

When Francine came down for breakfast, I took a quick, discreet look, standing over her briefly while she ate her cereal. What I saw made me want to scream. Her hair was *full* of lice; they were everywhere.

"Oh, honey, it looks like you've got something in your hair," I said, trying to stay calm. "You know, I think it might be . . . well, it looks like you might have a thing we call head lice. Don't worry. It's no big deal. We'll take care of it. You'll be fine."

I rushed to the store and bought a box of RID, then used the kit's fine-tooth comb to get the hundreds, or more accurately, thousands—maybe even *millions*—of nits out of Francine's very, very thick, shoulder-length black hair. It was such an ordeal, I silently prayed as I worked that I wouldn't have to do this job more than once.

Little did I know!

I called the exchange students' adviser at school to alert her to the possibility that the other exchange students—and their host families—might have lice as well. *Then* it occurred to me that I should check the rest of our kids too. That's when the real nightmare began.

We *all* had head lice. Even Sam, who was still a baby. And even Don and I had them!

(Can you imagine what it was like for me during this ordeal to perform in concert, standing up there on stage with my fancy show clothes and makeup on, thinking, *I hope no one finds out I have head lice?*)

An unbelievably intense ritual soon began: Every day for a week or so, as soon as the kids came home from school, I would wash their hair in the sink, comb it out, then use the little fine-tooth comb to pull out any nits. Next I would spray their hair with Lysol (yes, Lysol), put a plastic bag over their hair, wrap their head in a towel, and park them in front of the television for two hours.

Don and I treated each other and finally managed to conquer our lice. But for the kids, the misery was just beginning.

These were the days when the red bag had to go back and forth between the kids' dad's house and our house. I told their dad about the lice and sent along the RID kits, but despite everyone's best efforts, we just could not get those lice to die. They would seem to go away, then I'd do a random check and find that they had reappeared.

School ended, Francine went home, summer began, and the head lice continued.

One of the problems (I know now) is that I was doing the "hair thing" very thoroughly, but I wasn't following the rest of the instructions on the RID bottle and other guidelines I found online. Finally I wised up and performed the full, exhausting ritual. In addition to the hair-washing, spraying, bagging, and combing, every morning when the kids got up, I also stripped their beds, put the sheets and pillowcases in a plastic bag and sprayed them thoroughly with Lysol, tied the bag, and put it in the basement where it would stay three weeks to let the death-spray work. Then I sprayed their mattresses and the carpet around their beds.

One week I went room by room, taking everything out of every drawer and giving it the same treatment as the bedding. To this day whenever I smell Lysol or bleach, I think, *Head lice.*

We finally got the boys' infestation under control by cutting off all their hair. But for the girls, especially Aly and Jenn with their long, silky tresses, the head lice lived on.

You're only supposed to use RID every two weeks, as I recall. Soon, like a possessed madwoman, I started using it every day. I started checking the kids before they came into the house, washing the infected kids' hair outside with the garden hose, and combing out the nits before they came inside. Then I would bring them into the mudroom and make them take off all their clothes and put on new ones.

We cleaned out backpacks. We didn't wear hats or ball caps. We sprayed *everything* with Lysol, washed *everything* in bleach, and easily could have used a tanker-truckload of RID. We did so much laundry, I'm sure our water bill doubled. Finally, after what seemed like *years* of agony, we got rid of the head lice. Thank You, Jesus! The head lice went away just as my mind was starting to disappear as well.

Now, just let me take a moment here to point out a lesson I learned from the head-lice calamity. It's a perfect example of how we learn from our mistakes, and it applies to life as well as lice. You don't want to admit you have head lice, just as you probably don't want to admit you have sin in your life. Once that sin is identified, however, and you decide to get serious about cleaning up your act—decide that you're really going to get rid of the junk in your life, such as addiction, a toxic relationship, or whatever it may be, then you have to do a *thorough* cleansing. You can't do it halfway, as I did when I was treating the kids' hair but not their clothes and bedding.

You have to read the directions. For Christians, those directions are found in the Bible. Read it, study it, and learn from it. For moms treating their kids' head lice, the directions are on the bottle of RID and on the Internet. I read part of the directions, but I didn't read them all. As a result, my family spent a lot more time in head-lice land than we should have.

· ·

—Life in the Blender

Guilty Pleasures

● ● ● Luci Swindoll

Once, when I was on yet another diet, I asked Marilyn to help me watch my weight, especially with sweets, for which I have a fatal weakness. During the first couple of weeks, everything went great. Lots of fish, chicken, cottage cheese, and lettuce. But on my way home from work one afternoon, I had an uncontrollable urge to drive by that Baskin-Robbins ice cream parlor near my house. *Life's too short*, I thought, *to never have ice cream again.* In no time I was lapping around the edge of a large scoop of "chocolate 'n' peanut butter" on a lightly toasted sugar cone. Heavenly!

Later that evening, after Marilyn and I did a little shopping, I jokingly asked her if she'd like to stop by the ice cream parlor for a cone. Without the slightest hesitation, she responded, "Great idea! I was just thinking how delicious one would taste right now. Besides, you've been so good all this time, you deserve it. Come on, I'll buy."

As guilty as I felt, I just *couldn't* tell her. We drove along in silence, Marilyn no doubt relishing the idea of savoring ice cream, me praying fervently that the woman who waited on me earlier was no longer on duty. We got our ice cream (a different saleswoman was at the counter) and sat in the car, munching, licking, and making small talk. Then the brilliant idea hit me that it might be fun to confess my sin in some creative way. So I turned to Marilyn and said, "Hey, Mar, if you can tell me what I'm thinking about this Baskin-Robbins store, I'll take you to see that musical we've been wanting to go to."

"What? Is that it? No hints?"

"No hints. You get three guesses. Come on, Mar, you can do it. Just guess what I'm thinking."

"Fat chance." I winced when she said that. "Okay, Luci, my first guess is that you've decided to have your picture made right here in front of the store for your new book. Everybody will see how festive you are and will want to buy the book."

"Great guess! That's fabulous! It's wrong, but it's such a good guess!"

After a few more minutes of intense concentration, Marilyn said, "All right. My second guess is that you have made arrangements to work in this ice cream parlor for one week in order to gather stories for your book. Right?"

I grinned again. "Wrong again, pal. But your guesses are so vivid. Shows you're *really* using the ol' imagination."

Suddenly, she blurted out, "This is outrageous, I know, but since I only have one more guess, I'll shoot in the dark. Here's number three: You've already been in here once today for ice cream. Chocolate. You didn't want to tell me earlier because you were embarrassed since you had asked me to help you stick to your diet. And then when I answered yes when you asked if I wanted to come here, you were so caught off guard that you decided to go along with it anyway like nothing had happened. That's why you ordered lemon ice cream. You already had chocolate once today. Besides, lemon is nearer your diet, and you thought I'd be proud of you if I heard you order lemon instead of chocolate."

I stared at her with my half-eaten cone poised in midair. "Well???"

"Marilyn, this is *unreal*! I can't believe it! How did you guess that? I'*m* the only one who could know all those details. Boy, is this spooky. A regular Steven Spielberg production."

She was roaring with laughter. It seems that the woman who had waited on me earlier in the day was the mother of a school friend of Marilyn's daughter, Beth. In a casual conversation at the grocery store, the woman innocently mentioned to Marilyn that I had been in that afternoon for an ice cream cone. She had recognized me from church and knew that Marilyn and I were friends. Marilyn decided not to mention the incident to me but thought she'd beat me at my own game. What an imagination that woman has! She played along from start to finish! I loved it!

Let your imagination run wild and think up new ways to add spice to your life.

． ．

—*You Bring the Confetti, God Brings the Joy*

The Perils of Exercise

● ● ● Barbara Johnson

All hard work brings a profit, but mere
talk leads only to poverty.
—Proverbs 14:23

*D*ear Barbara,
My doctor insists that I must begin a vigorous exercise program. Can you suggest one?
Plump in Petoskey

Dear Plump,
The most important thing to remember about exercise is to start SLOWLY . . . and then taper off. And remember this: The easiest way to get a healthy body is to MARRY one!

● ● ●

There *is* one exercise that I tried, and it sounded so simple . . . I was supposed to bend over my vacuum cleaner and extend my right leg behind me while I touched my head to my knee. This was just before my vacuum sucked up my nightgown and caused me to completely pass out!

I had to give up jogging for my health . . . My thighs kept rubbing together and setting my pantyhose on fire!

—*Daily Splashes of Joy*

Nonsense in Their Veins

● ● ● Luci Swindoll

I love being around people who seem to have non-sense in their veins. They're the ones who erase tension in business meetings, liven up a schoolroom or office discussion, and relieve boredom wherever they go. If you have someone like that in your life, you need to stop right now and thank God, because that person is a beautiful gift straight from heaven. Anne Lamott says, "Nothing gives hope like laughter. It moisturizes the soul." The difficulties of life break down into manageable sizes. It's a "momentary anesthesia of the heart," to quote French philosopher Henri Bergson.

All my "Porch Pals" on the Women of Faith speaking team value a sense of humor as much as I, and each of them has a razor-sharp wit. Their ability to find laughter in life was actually a prerequisite for joining the team. When we first started working for this ministry, we were simply told to "make 'em laugh"—and that's one thing we've enjoyed doing ever since. Of course, we also have to say something of value, but the ability to find humor in tough times and to encourage others to do the same is still high on our priority list.

Interestingly, research shows that laughter itself serves no biological purpose. It's a reflex action, sometimes called a "luxury reflex," unrelated to humanity's struggle for survival. Yet the emotional service it provides can't begin to be measured. According to Proverbs 17:22, laughter is "good medicine," and we've all experienced a healthy dose of that medicine when we didn't even know we were sick. Laughter lifts our spirit and drops the fever. Somehow, it opens the windows to our soul, letting in light and fresh air. A friend of mine used to say, "Laughter is kind of like changing my baby's diaper—it doesn't solve any problems permanently, but it certainly makes things more enjoyable at the moment."

....

—Life! Celebrate It

Find the Joy!

● ● ● Sandi Patty

The apostle Paul said, "You'll do best by filling your minds and meditating on things true, noble, reputable, authentic, compelling, gracious—the best, not the worst; the beautiful, not the ugly, things to praise, not things to curse" (Philippians 4:8 MSG). I love that verse, but honestly, I think it has been my kids who have helped me most to fill my mind and meditate on "the beautiful, not the ugly." After all, they're the ones who are constantly reminding me, in their laughter-sprinkled, teasing voices, "Find the joy, Mom! You've gotta find the joy!"

They've even given me one of their own attitude-adjustment items to add to my thankfulness list. They say, "We're thankful to have a curfew (although we always wish it could be later), because it means someone cares about us."

I'm thankful my kids can still teach their mom a thing or two.

Of course, there's always at least one jokester in the group ready to make some wisecrack about my positive perspective and grateful attitude. When I was on a long road trip last year, I called home and told Sam I would be so glad to see him, that when I got back I would kiss him all over his face.

He was quiet for a minute and finally said, "Uh, Mom? Are you gonna have lipstick on? Because I don't want that stuff all over me."

—Life in the Blender

My Favorite Excuse

● ● ● Barbara Johnson

> Be truly glad! There is wonderful joy ahead, even
> though the going is rough for a while down here.
> These trials are only to test your faith.
> —1 Peter 1:6 TLB

We can hope for a miracle, but there is no simple, quick way to be young, thin, and lovely. As the years zoom by, you begin to think you're in a war to keep your mind together, your body functioning, your teeth in, your hair on, and your weight off. It can really be a chore. It's a lot like trying to hold a beachball under water . . . sooner or later something pops up or out! That's why my favorite excuse is, "I used to be Snow White . . . but I drifted!"

Aging gracefully means living long enough to make a joke
of the things that were once breaking your heart.

— *Daily Splashes of Joy*

Part 6

Get Outta Here!

Laughing at Life's Ridiculous Moments

• • • • •

Real friends are those who, when you've
made a fool of yourself, don't think you've
done a permanent job.

On an Olympic Scale, I'd Give It a 7.4

● ● ●   Ann Luna

I was returning a book to a certain relative's house, and he wasn't home. If he had been home like he was supposed to have been, none of this would have happened.

I left the book on the table, and as I headed back down the driveway, I couldn't help but notice that his tomato vines were drooping with large, red orbs shining in the sun. As one who is addicted to home-grown tomatoes, there was no way I could just drive by that struggling garden without stopping to help. Those poor plants were going to break off and sustain serious injuries if something wasn't done, and soon.

My relative had told me I could help myself to tomatoes anytime I wanted. Or maybe he had said, "God help you if you step foot in my garden one more time." I can't quite remember. Anyway, the tomatoes were calling me, and no one was watching, and I figured he surely wouldn't miss just a few. Dozen.

The problem was that he had built a pen around his tomato patch that would rival the security around Fort Knox. He had used sheet metal wired onto rebar stakes to keep out the armadillos—and possibly to keep me out too. I mean, the darn armadillos aren't even a foot high, so why does the sheet metal have to come nearly up to my thighs? From a distance, the fence looked like a cute little bit of rectangular yard art decorating the hilltop. Up close, I felt like an illegal immigrant staring up at the wall guarding the border into Texas.

I gripped the treacherous edge of the sheet metal with both hands as I grunted and groaned while hoisting my arthritic knees over the barricade, glad no one could see that I had lost just a tiny bit of my youthful agility. My mouth was already watering as I hurriedly pulled several large, juicy tomatoes off the vines. Then, clutching my treasures against my stomach, I turned to face the prison wall.

Unable to use my hands because they were cradling my precious contraband, I teetered unsteadily on one foot and threw the other one up and *almost* over the sheet metal. I was halfway there, already dreaming of being alone with nothing but the tomatoes and a salt shaker, when I shifted a bit and my earthbound pants leg got caught on one of the rebar stakes. My brain sent out an emergency message to my arms to frantically fling themselves out so I could catch myself. But another part of my brain was screaming, *No! Don't drop the tomatoes!*

As a result, I clutched the tomatoes against my shirt, turning them into ketchup as the top half of my body tilted backward and my airborne leg whirled around in a lopsided arc that must have looked like a complicated Ferris wheel–helicopter maneuver.

It's hard to imagine now, but I was a cheerleader in high school, and back then, doing cartwheels and somersaults was as easy as falling off a log. Thirty-some years and twenty-some pounds later, falling off a log—or over a fence—is a whole 'nuther ball game.

I would never have believed I could still do the splits.

But I did.

When my high-flying leg finally decided to come in for a

landing, it swung forward and slid down the sheet metal, grinding itself over the tops of the stakes until it finally bounced to a stop. Meanwhile, the pant leg that was stuck on the rebar had torn itself loose in all the excitement, so I was now free to follow my other leg down to the ground, banging and clanging against the metal as I descended.

They say your life passes before your eyes as you encounter life-changing events, but my life has been way too short to fill the time it took me to go through all the gyrations preceding my final impact. Instead, I had a progression of thoughts that began with, *Oh! I'm going to crush the tomatoes!* and moved on to, *Gee, I wonder if I'll need stitches*, before ending with, *I hope my family knows I want that powder-blue casket at the funeral home.*

Lying there in the tomato patch with tweety-birds circling my head and stars flashing on and off in my brain, I at first thought the rebar had completely punctured my leg and I had skewered myself like a big tomato-and-beef kabob. Then I realized the blood that covered my body was actually tomato juice.

Only then did I come close to tears, when I realized I had smashed the tomatoes. Not to mention that I'd put a bit of a dent in my relative's Alcatraz-style tomato-protection system. And wouldn't you know? Despite all my Olympic-style acrobatics and high-altitude leg twirling, I had still landed *inside* the fence.

Defeated, I grieved a moment over the now-shapeless tomatoes embedded in my shirt, gripped the now-sagging sheet metal with my now-empty hands, eased my now-red-white-and-blue body carefully over the fence, and limped back to the car.

Like the ancient mariner who was forced to wear around his neck the albatross he had killed, I now wear the scars of my tomato-patch thievery on my leg: baseball-size knots and bruises bulging from my calf, and a deep, zipperlike scratch that runs from my knee to my ankle. People gasp when they see these wounds, so at first I tried to wear long pants to spare them the shock. But the Neosporin sticks to the fabric, and it's just too hot for long pants. Next I wore shorts and tried to make up lies to explain the unsightly injuries. But that didn't work either. No one believed I'd been hit by an RPG while serving with the marines in Baghdad, and when I tried the snake-bite alibi, a woman at the supermarket said, "Did one snake bite you three times, or did three snakes get you all at once?"

Now I'm just trying to stay home until the bruises disappear—or at least until they turn yellow so they're less noticeable. I'm also trying to be on my best behavior, and I'm staying out of the barricaded tomato patch. I'm hoping that, once he gets the new concertina wire installed, my relative will realize the error of his ways and just *bring* me some tomatoes, for heaven's sake.

Surprised by Doubt

● ● ● Sheila Walsh

I wonder how many people have walked away from a relationship with God because their inner doubts and questions have overwhelmed and isolated them. They live with the fallout of unanswered questions. I met such a woman on a weekend when it seemed as if everything that could go wrong did go wrong on our trip to Shreveport, Louisiana, in 2003.

We started out from Nashville fairly early in the morning; if all had gone as planned, we would have been in Shreveport in the early afternoon. We were supposed to fly through Dallas, but it was experiencing some very bad weather. So, after a three-hour wait in Nashville, our flight was rerouted through St. Louis. By the time we got to our hotel it was almost 11:30. Usually there are one or two bellmen waiting to help with bags, but our hotel had no bellmen—and no luggage carts. Poor Barry had to haul ten large pieces of luggage upstairs by himself as I carried a very sleepy six-year-old boy.

We hadn't had a chance to eat, so after we got Christian settled, I looked to see if there was a late-night menu in the hotel. Room service had closed at ten o'clock. Barry said he was starving, so I called Domino's Pizza. We waited for about forty minutes, and there was still no aroma of pepperoni in the air, so I called to check on the order. An extremely harried man told me that he hadn't even started on our order.

"It's a joke!" he said. "It's a bad joke. I'm all by myself. Bill is sick and Frank quit, so I'm all alone."

"I'm so sorry!" I said. "Tell Bill we hope he feels better soon. Just forget the pizza. We're so tired now anyway."

"No, ma'am," he said. "You ordered a pizza, and a pizza you shall have!"

The pizza arrived an hour and twenty minutes later. By that time Christian was asleep, Barry was asleep, and I had a pizza the size of Texas.

The next morning Barry went to the arena to set up, and Christian and I read a few books, then left the room for an hour to let the housekeeping staff clean. We decided to go downstairs for lunch but were advised that the restaurant closed at eleven in the morning and wouldn't be open till five that afternoon. Christian had said that he wasn't hungry until he found out that the restaurant was closed—then he informed me that he was starving to death.

I called Barry on his cell phone to advise him that we had landed in a food wasteland, and he should grab something at the arena if he could. He said that he would come back and take Christian to lunch at a local spot a few blocks away. That way I could shower and get over to the arena for my sound check. Once they had headed off, I went back to my room. When I opened the door I saw that the room was clean, but there were no towels. I approached one of the housekeeping staff who was pushing a cart along our floor. "I don't seem to have any towels, ma'am," I said.

"I know, baby," she replied kindly. "We're all out of towels."

"You have no towels?"

"Not a dry one in the house."

"When do you think you'll have some?"

"Could be this afternoon—could be tonight. Lord only knows! They're trying to wash them."

I went back into my room to think about which one of Barry's shirts I could dry myself on. I sat down on the chair by the bed and it promptly collapsed under me, dumping me in a heap on the floor. (I knew I shouldn't have eaten that pizza!) I called Barry and told him that I would have to skip my sound check and find a towel. I went back down to the lobby to ask if they could rustle up just one, even a little one, even a partially used towel or a very fluffy cat! They promised they would send something up.

I was waiting for an elevator back to my room when I heard a woman's voice behind me say, "I suppose you're back with more faith?"

I turned to see if she was talking to me and saw immediately by the intensity of her stare that she was. "Excuse me?" I said.

"Aren't you with that faith group?" she asked.

"I'm with Women of Faith," I replied.

"That's the one I meant. I've been to one of your conferences," she continued.

I got the decided feeling that it had not been a good experience for her. "Are you coming tonight?"

"No, I'm not coming," she said.

"I'd be glad to get you tickets," I said, wondering if cost was an issue for her.

"No, thanks. I used to be very involved in the church, but I don't go anymore."

"Do you mind if I ask why?" I said.

"I used to believe. I used to believe that God loved me, and the church would be there for you when times got rough, but it's a crock. The church is just a building full of people pretending to be okay when they're bleeding to death."

With that she turned and left. I followed her out the front door of the hotel, but she was gone. I felt such an ache as I stared across an empty parking lot. I heard her words, but more than that, I heard her heart. I heard the pain and disappointment, and I wondered what her story was. All I could do was pray for her.

Pray—surely that is the greatest thing we can do for each other, but I think sometimes we need the hug of flesh and blood. I know that at my most painful moments in life I have wanted to see eyes look back at me with compassion and understanding: God present in outstretched arms and listening ears. I wondered if she had any place to take her doubt, her questions, or would that be too risky? How many people have walked away from the church because they didn't dare say out loud what was going on in their hearts?

As believers we find it easy to share what we perceive to be our great moments of faith or insight, but we usually keep our doubts to ourselves. . . . I believe that doubts, honestly expressed and wrestled with, produce a faith that is stronger and more intimate than doubts suppressed under the veneer of faith.

. . . .

—*Extraordinary Faith*

Climb In, Little Piggy?

● ● ● Max Lucado

id I just read what I think I read? I drove around the block for a second glance. The announcement, taped to a stop-sign pole, had a home computer look to it: yellow paper and thick letters. Our neighbors, like yours, print and post all types of fliers. The presence of the announcement didn't surprise me, but the words did.

FOUND: POTBELLIED PIG

Two phone numbers followed: one to call during the day and another to call at night. I'd never seen such an announcement. Similar ones, sure.

FOUND: BLACK RETRIEVER
FOUND: PSYCHEDELIC SKATEBOARD
FOUND: GOLD BROOCH

But "Found: Potbellied Pig"? Who loses a pig? Who *owns* a pig?

I know many pet owners, but pet-pig owners? Can you imagine providing daily care for a pig? (Denalyn says she can.) Do pig owners invite dinner guests to pet the pig? Do they hang a sign on the outside gate: "Potbelly on Patrol"? Pig owners must be a special breed.

Even more so, those who rescue them. The sign presupposes a curious moment. Someone spotted the pig lumbering down the sidewalk. "Poor thing. Climb in, little piggy, piggy, piggy. The street is no place for a lonely sow. I'll take you home."

Suppose one appeared on your porch. Upon hearing a snort at your front door, would you open it? Not me. Golden retriever? You bet. German shepherd? Will do. St. Bernard? Count on me for a few nights and a few neighborhood signs. But a potbellied pig? Sorry. I'd leave him on Jericho Road.

I wouldn't claim one. But God would. God did. God did when He claimed us.

. . . .

—*Come Thirsty*

Spending Christmas with a Rodent

● ● ● Mary Graham

> Cast all your anxiety on him because
> he cares for you.
> —1 Peter 5:7

*E*normous problems don't upset me. I take on challenges as if mountains were easily scaled. When an opportunity comes, I typically bite off more than I can chew. When I see the unthinkable, it makes me want to trust God and believe Him for a miracle. Little things, however . . .

Some time ago, I was babysitting Christian Walsh's pets. His family was on a trip to Scotland; so I volunteered to keep the family menagerie, which at the time was only Belle, the dog, and Hamtaro, the hamster. I don't really understand anything at all about hamsters, but I'm crazy about Christian and would do anything he asked, including spending Christmas with a rodent.

It couldn't have been easier, until on the ninth day, early in the morning, I saw no sign of life in the hamster cage and realized I'd seen nothing the day before either. For one dizzy moment, I thought, *Maybe the little fellow's been asleep for a couple of days.* I ran to the nearest computer and Googled the question: "Do hamsters hibernate?"

Immediately, the response came, "Only in the wild."

Shoot! So I phoned my friend Cindy, who knows everything about dogs, thinking perhaps her dog knowledge could apply to all animals. I left her a message. Then I remembered a friend whose son had received two hamsters as a gift. After her son bonded to them, they discovered they had one male and one female, which accidentally resulted in a family of twenty hamsters in their household. So I left a message on her cell phone—surely she'd know what to do.

I decided if Hamtaro was dead in the cage, I'd take the whole thing—cage and critter—to the pet shop from which it came and ask them to do an autopsy. I wanted to ensure that he would have died anyway, even if he'd been in Christian's care.

I obsessed on this for several hours until my brave little friend, Patsy Clairmont (who happened to be staying with me at the time), awakened. Although Patsy shares freely about the huge part fear played in her life as a young girl, in this instance she was the picture of strength and exactly what I needed. She courageously opened the cage and found not a *dead* hamster but *no* hamster at all.

"Honey," she said softly, "there's no hamster in this cage." As the mother of two sons, Patsy understood the hamster species; so she started crawling around on the floor looking in nooks and crannies. I did nothing but wring my hands. And then it hit me: we had two dogs in the house! Mine and Belle. That's it—Hamtaro's history! I knew we could really be facing a disaster here, and Christian was due home in less than twenty-four hours.

Finally, Patsy spotted a very frightened little Hamtaro under the washing machine and delivered him safely back into his cage. All was well. We celebrated with great joy!

It was then I remembered that *all* the promises of God are true, *all* the time. He can *always* be trusted. He's *always* there. He doesn't judge our requests, feelings, needs, fears, desires, inadequacies, insecurities, or vulnerabilities. He doesn't leave us on our own when our issues are too minor or too impossible to manage. He doesn't say, "I don't do hamsters."

Instead, He takes care to call us His children, His beloved, His friends. He says to us, "Come to Me." I've never seen a verse, passage, or intonation in His Word that says, "Go away. Come back when you have a real need or when I have more time."

. . . .

—*Contagious Joy*

Saving My Satin Pillows

● ● ● Marilyn Meberg

A cat shows up at the pearly gates of heaven.

St. Peter: I know you! You were a very nice cat on earth and didn't cause any trouble, so I want to offer a gift to you of one special thing you have always wanted.

Cat: Well, I did always long to own a nice satin pillow like my master had, so I could lie on it.

St. Peter: That's easy. Granted. You shall have the satin pillow after you enter in.

Next a group of mice appear.

St. Peter: Ah, I remember you! You were such good mice on earth. You didn't steal food from anyone's house and never hurt other animals. Therefore, I want to grant you one special wish you always wanted.

The Chief Mouse: Well, we always watched the children playing and saw them roller-skate. It was beautiful, and it looked like so much fun. So can we each have some roller skates, please?

St. Peter: Granted. You shall have your wish.

The next day, St. Peter is making rounds inside the gates and sees the cat.

St. Peter: Well, Cat, did you enjoy the satin pillow?

Cat: Oh, indeed I did. And say, that Meals-on-Wheels thing was a nice touch too!

I love satin pillows—they are soft, smooth, and luxurious rewards. Rewards for what? For the cat, for making it to heaven. For me, just for being alive. I have three huge satin pillows on my bed that please me enormously. I walk through the bedroom during the day and look over at them as they smile regally back at me. Just exchanging looks with them never fails to smooth my soul.

I suppose they are impractical, as I only use them for decoration. To haul them onto the floor for a quick sit or teensy lounge is unthinkable to me. It's just not an option. Why? I think it's because I sometimes suffer from the "save-it-for-later" syndrome. Maybe later I won't be so picky, or maybe later they won't look quite so gorgeous, or maybe later I could risk getting body lotion on one of them. In spite of being a confirmed "now" person, I occasionally have little lapses that don't make sense—like saving my satin pillows for . . . who knows when!

What I'm about to say will probably give you whiplash, but I'm going to risk your neck and say it anyway. I think the experience of God-ordained marital submission could be a satin pillow for you. If your husband is conscientiously seeking God's sufficiency in his own life and thus in yours, you can start to relax. You can start to feel secure and cared for. That's God's planned pattern for you. Stretch out on a satin pillow and know your needs are known and cared about.

Now, of course, the Proverbs 31 woman (who can make us all a little tight-jawed) did not spend her days lolling around on a pillow. She worked like a Trojan and was praised for doing so. But if God's pattern was accepted in her life, she was on that pillow—perhaps not literally, but figuratively. Her soul was smoothed on her satin reward. She was working and accomplishing, but she knew she was loved and honored.

Being loved and honored is the pillow part. You may be excessively busy, or you may be sitting with tea and pound cake. In any case, your soul needs smoothing. Receiving God's pattern for your marriage is a great reward. Don't save it for later.

. . . .

—Since You Asked

God's Garden

● ● ● Patsy Clairmont

God's seeds of hope are often sown by people and books. For me, Rose was used by God to plant a garden of hope in my heart.

I met Rose over the telephone, which seemed prophetic since we would end up spending years of our friendship with phones dangling from our ears, as we conversed about God, husbands, children, and ministry. Rose helped me start a Bible study in my home and invited me to join her staff at a local women's retreat when I was in my late twenties. Her gentle approach and her spacious, grace-driven heart offered me a sheltered atmosphere to grow in.

I remember the time Rose prayed God would give me an FM radio so I could listen to her favorite Bible teachers. I thought asking God for a radio was ludicrous. But faith-filled Rose was steadfast in her prayer efforts. Every few days she would call, and our conversations would unfold something like this:

"Well?" Rose would respond to my "hello."

"Hi, Rose. Well what?"

"Did you get an FM radio yet?"

"No, Rose. And it's not likely to happen, you know. We don't have the money to buy a radio."

"Oh, Patsy, I know that. But God's gonna provide. You'll see; I'll just keep praying."

I'd hang up and roll my eyes. Yeah, right, an FM radio sponsored by God. Uh-huh.

Then one day Les rushed into the house. "Patsy, come here; I have a surprise!" I followed him out to a large rental truck. He threw open the door and there, all alone in the cavern, was a long, television console. Some people had given it to Les for helping them out. It was lovely, and I was excited. I called Rose to tell her about it, but I heard disappointment in her voice. "What's wrong?" I asked.

"Oh, I thought you were going to tell me you had an FM radio," she confessed.

I screamed, "Rose, it has an AM-FM radio and stereo! It never hit me; this is God's answer to your prayer!"

Don't ask me how Rose knew God would do that, but she did. After that I wasn't so quick to discard any seeds she wanted to plant in me about God and prayer. I didn't have her mustard-seed faith; mine was more a granule of sand, but I learned to lean on her more mature faith while I was little in mine.

* *

—*I Grew Up Little*

Riding Shotgun with an Ex-Con Angel

● ● ● Ann Luna

*E*xcept for the tattoos, the tow truck driver, with his squinty blue eyes and dimpled smile, reminded my daughter Reagan and me of actor Kurt Russell in his younger years. Actually, after we had waited an hour in the broiling heat beside the interstate, anyone driving a tow truck would have looked good to us.

We had been traveling from Missouri to Florida and were in south Georgia late on a Sunday afternoon when the car broke down. It took the tow truck driver— I'll call him Kurt— less than sixty seconds to load the crippled car onto the flatbed. (Turns out he's a repo man on the side.)

I dug around for the center seat belt in the tow truck's cab but couldn't find it. So I insisted Reagan and I share the shoulder belt. When Kurt climbed into the driver's seat, he paused a moment to stare at the two women squished into the opposite corner, tied up like a tenderloin by the too-tight seat belt.

"Y'all decided to get friendly?" he said, his eyebrows raised.

"Well, I wanted us both to have a seat belt—and Kurt, I think you should wear yours too."

"No, ma'am," he said, smiling politely. "Last time I rolled a truck, I woulda been killed if I'd had a belt on. But I can dig out the center belt—unless y'all just like to sit close up like that."

We dug out the belt.

"Have you been busy this weekend?" I asked. We had to be towed 160 miles, and I thought a little chitchat would help pass the nearly three hours we would spend together.

"Unbelievable," Kurt answered. He waved a yellow pad filled with names and phone numbers of the people he had rescued. "I haven't had more than forty-five minutes' sleep since Friday."

"Are you sure you're up for such a long drive?" I asked worriedly. "Maybe you should get some rest and see if someone else can drive us."

"Oh, I've made it on lots less sleep than this," he said confidently. "No problem."

"Okay, but let's at least stop and get something to eat," I said. "Let me buy you a sandwich somewhere."

"I'll be glad to stop, but I can't eat," he said. "I got my tongue pierced on Thursday"—he stuck it out to show us the silver stud—"and it's so swollen I haven't been able to eat much of anything."

My brain slowly processed the information: We were going to ride 160 miles with a pierced and tattooed driver who had had forty-five minutes' sleep in the last forty-eight hours and who hadn't eaten anything since Thursday. He had rolled at least one truck and no telling how many others. I wanted to say, "Stop! Let me think a minute. Surely a better idea will come to me!"

But off we went, rumbling down the interstate, windows down since there was no air conditioning. Kurt drove with his left elbow resting on the window sill and his left hand propping up his head. His right arm extended straight out from the shoulder so that his wrist draped over the steering wheel.

Determined to keep him awake, I went into Suzy Reporter mode, asking every question I could think of. A few too many questions, as it turned out.

"You've probably seen some bad accidents out here on the interstate," I began.

"Yes ma'am. Worked a double fatality last week."

"People drive so fast," I said.

"Yes ma'am. I like to drive fast too. I was haulin' an RV on the interstate last year and got stopped for goin' ninety-two."

"You were going ninety-two miles per hour and towing an RV?" I shrieked, glancing at the speedometer. "How much was your ticket?"

"Seven hundred thirty-two dollars and four points off my license," he said, shaking his head. "I can't go that fast in this truck. It has a governor that tops out at sixty-five."

"Well, I'm glad to hear that," I said. Then, moving on to what I hoped would be a less stressful subject, I noted, "You've got a lot of interesting tattoos."

"Yes ma'am. Got 'em on my back and chest too."

"Wow. It must have hurt."

"Nah. Not too much. I did most of 'em myself."

"You did your own tattoos? Where did you learn to do that?"

Kurt was quiet a moment, probably wondering just how much more I could bear. Then he stared straight out the windshield and said, "San Quentin."

I gulped.

"San Quentin . . . the city?" I asked hopefully.

"California State Correctional Facility," he answered, his steely eyes still trained on the highway.

We rode in silence, all three of us now staring straight ahead as the terrifying thought filled my brain: *We are riding with a hungry, sleep-deprived, pierced and tattooed, speed-demon ax murderer, and we are all going to die.*

"Got messed up with drugs," Kurt said. "But I'm clean now."

Then Reagan, normally a brilliant young gal with a lot of common sense, asked Kurt, "What's the first thing you did when you got out?"

He leaned forward, turned his head toward her and grinned, then fixed his eyes back on the road. "After a man's been in prison six years, there's only one thing on his mind when he gets out. But I reckon your mama wouldn't want me talkin' about that right now."

I gave Reagan my most ferocious death-ray stare and hissed, "Shhhhh!"

After that I carefully focused the conversation on music preferences, fast-food favorites, and cars that Kurt admired. When we arrived at the dealership, I was never so happy to see my husband, Dave, waiting for us. But I was grateful to Kurt, too, and I insisted that Dave give him a good tip. He had gotten us and our crippled car to our destination safely, and our exciting conversation had made the time fly by. Now, as he waved and drove off, I thought of him in a whole new way: as a hungry, sleep-deprived, pierced and tattooed, speed-demon *angel* driving a tow truck.

Public Speaking, Cesspool-Style

● ● ● Barbara Johnson

*M*y years of public speaking have rewarded me with many blessings. One of them is that I've met many very creative women. . . . for me, this is one of the greatest rewards of undertaking this rather risky adventure. For example, soon after my book *Splashes of Joy in the Cesspools of Life* came out, I was invited to speak at a large banquet at a megachurch in Arizona. As we walked into the banquet room, we were shocked—and delighted—at what we saw.

The room had been decorated "cesspool style," one of the clever women laughingly told us. Rolls of pink, yellow, blue, and white toilet tissue had been gracefully draped all around the banquet room, and streamers of the tissue formed a wistful curtain to hide the edge of the speakers platform. And on the platform were three complete toilets covered with gold paper and sparkly stuff—truly a sight to behold. Each of the fifty tables was set with a rubber-plunger centerpiece covered with pink feathers, white pearls, and toilet-tissue bows. Can you imagine the fun we had in such a setting?

To start things off, the director of women's ministry stood up and said, "Let's plunge right in, ladies!" Then she taught us a little song: "Flush away, flush away, flush away all," and the place fairly rocked with all the gals laughing, singing, swinging, and swaying.

The crowning joy of the day was the farewell gift the ladies gave us—a lovely toilet seat encrusted with pearls and trimmed with feathers, sprayed all over with more sparklies. Bill hand-carried it all the way back to California, and you can believe he was the talk of the airport that day! Of all the places we've been and all the conferences we've been a part of, THAT was certainly the most memorable decor. It still makes me laugh just to think of it.

After another speaking appearance, we got a splash of joy from a letter written by one of the women attending. She commended the organizers of the Joyful Journey tour, a nationwide series of women's conferences that I participated in. The woman said she appreciated how everything had been planned right down to the smallest detail—even to having Scripture verses taped to the back of the restroom doors! She noted, however, that the Scripture verse she had found in her restroom stall had been "a little unsettling," It read, "YOU ARE SURROUNDED BY SO GREAT A CLOUD OF WITNESSES"!

. . . .

—*Living Somewhere Between Estrogen and Death*

Luci's Law

● ● ● Luci Swindoll

e've all read Murphy's Laws, and no doubt we've seen many of them in action. There seems to be one to cover every conceivable situation. They're funny because they're so true.

For example, "If there are two events of importance, they will always conflict." Haven't you thought that on the night two of your favorite movies were being aired on television at the same time on different channels? There are other old laws to live by that bear repeating:

Blake's Law: The longer you save something for future possible use, the sooner you need it after it's destroyed.

Roe's Law. No matter what happens, somebody knew it would.

Childer's Law: When everything is perfectly clear to everyone, somebody didn't get the message.

Donsen's Law: The specialist learns more and more about less and less until he knows everything about nothing.

Which brings me to my own law:

Swindoll's Law: Leaders who always have to do the job themselves often do a job on themselves.

—*Notes to a Working Woman*

The Problems Started with the Birthday Cake

● ● ● Ann Luna

Dear Esther,

I'm sorry you couldn't make it to my recent birthday party.

Apparently it was quite an event—not that I remember much about it.

They tell me the problems started when I drew in a big breath to blow out the eighty-four candles someone had set afire on top of my birthday cake and, blinded by the glaring blaze and disoriented by the merciless heat, I forgot why I was holding my breath and temporarily lost consciousness.

Luckily, my daughter and her family had decided to host the party beside their swimming pool, so instead of breaking my hip in a disastrous fall to the kitchen floor, I toppled backward into the pool. The water was so cold, I instantly awakened from my faint, screaming at the top of my lungs and, as a result, losing my dentures in the deep end of the pool.

Without a moment's hesitation, my nephew Joey dived in and swam to the bottom to retrieve my teeth, but when he tried to resurface, he accidentally became entangled in the billowing fabric of my tent-shaped housedress, and together we kicked and flapped and squawked, undulating repeatedly until my wig finally let go and floated off, ghostlike, in the churning water.

Thinking one of her puppies was drowning, the old dog Sparky jumped in next, swimming determinedly into the fray to rescue the wig.

It was about that time that my birthday cake, with all seven dozen candles still burning, suddenly ignited like a sparkler and set the paper tablecloth on fire.

Fortunately, the firefighters arrived within minutes, and if the firetruck had been hauling water, I suppose everything would have turned out okay. But the truck's tanks were empty, so one of the firefighters, his yellow rubber coat popping and squeaking loudly as he ran, dropped a pumper hose in the pool.

I thought for sure he would rescue us, as we were still flapping and squawking in the icy water, but Sparky apparently mistook him for some sort of monster—perhaps a loud and lurching fire hydrant—and she suddenly began barking so ferociously that the poor man dropped the hose and never looked back. He said later he wondered why the old dog was so zealously guarding that undulating mass of inflatable beach toys.

Eventually, the pumping lowered the water level in the pool until our feet could touch bottom. But by then the whole backyard was a swirling vortex of flames and smoke. I couldn't see a thing, what with all the haze and chaos—and the fact that one lens of my bifocals had popped out when I hit the water. But Sparky obviously has either sharp eyesight or a keen memory despite her many years. She took off like a rocket after that same poor firefighter and took a big chunk out of his thigh before he scrambled up the only tree in the yard that wasn't burning.

I guess Joey and I looked a little bedraggled as we groped our way out of the pool and through the swirling curtain of smoke and chaos. We tried to slip, unseen, out of the growing crowd, but the firefighters mistook us for arsonists trying to avoid detection and quickly called the police, who were already en route in response to another call about a crazed and rabid dog wreaking havoc on our property.

I tried to explain what had happened, but since Joey had left my dentures back in the pool, no one could understand a word I was saying. They hauled us both off to jail, bringing Sparky along as a material witness.

It was nearly midnight before my daughter and her husband finally came to bail us out. I was surprised when they dropped me off at the YWCA, saying I would have to stay there for a little while. It was a little sad to think I had completely missed celebrating my birthday.

I hope you're doing well. Please give my regards to everyone at the nursing home. I'll try to give you plenty of notice next year so you can join me for a piece of birthday cake—if my daughter's house is rebuilt by then.

—Gertrude

Trying Not to Hiss

● ● ● Marilyn Meberg

A friend of mine took these instructions from the Internet and passed them on to me. Just in case you missed them, I'll share this bit of pertinent wisdom with you!

Instructions for Giving Your Cat a Pill

1. Pick cat up and cradle it in the crook of your left arm as if holding a baby. Position right forefinger and thumb on either side of cat's mouth and gently apply pressure to cheeks while holding pill in right hand. As cat opens mouth, pop pill into mouth. Help cat to close mouth and swallow.

2. Retrieve pill from floor and cat from behind sofa. Cradle cat in left arm and repeat process.

3. Retrieve cat from bedroom and throw soggy pill away.

4. Take new pill from foil wrap; cradle cat in left arm holding rear paws tightly with left hand. Force jaws open and push pill to back of mouth with right forefinger. Hold cat down for a count of ten.

5. Retrieve pill from goldfish bowl and cat from top of wardrobe. Call spouse from garden.

6. Kneel on floor with cat wedged firmly between knees, holding front and rear paws. Ignore low growls emitted by cat. Get spouse to hold cat's head firmly with one hand while

forcing wooden ruler into mouth. Drop pill down ruler and rub cat's throat vigorously.

7. Retrieve cat from curtain rail; get another pill from foil wrap. Make a note to buy a new ruler and repair curtains. Carefully sweep shattered figurines from mantel and set to one side for gluing later.

8. Wrap cat in large towel and get spouse to lie on cat with its head just visible from below spouse's armpit. Put pill in end of drinking straw, force cat's mouth open with pencil, and blow down drinking straw.

9. Check label to make sure pill not harmful to humans; drink glass of water to take taste away. Apply Band-Aid to spouse's forearm and remove blood from carpet with cold water and soap.

10. Retrieve cat from neighbor's shed. Get another pill. Place cat in cupboard and close door onto neck to leave head showing. Force mouth open with dessert spoon. Flick pill down throat with elastic band.

11. Fetch screwdriver from garage and put door back on hinges. Apply cold compress to cheek and check records for date of last tetanus shot. Throw T-shirt away and get new one from bedroom.

12. Ring fire department to retrieve cat from tree across the road. Apologize to neighbor who crashed into fence while swerving to avoid cat. Take last pill from foil wrap.

13. Tie cat's front paws to rear paws with garden twine and bind tightly to leg of dining table. Find heavy-duty pruning gloves from shed. Force cat's mouth open with small wrench. Push pill into mouth followed by large piece of filet mignon. Hold head vertically and pour half-pint of water down throat to wash pill down.

14. Get spouse to drive you to emergency room; sit quietly while doctor stitches fingers and forearm and removes

pill remnants from right eye. Stop by furniture store to order new table.

15. Arrange for vet to make a house call.

If you've lived to tell your own experience in medicating a pet, you could conclude that this instruction list is not far from the truth. In addition to giving me a giggle and pulling up childhood memories of my perennially depressed cat, Jeremiah, I find myself identifying with that feline resistance. Now of course I'm too civilized to hiss, spit, and break furniture, but there are certain left-hearted inclinations I don't want to accept, and I don't want anyone else addressing my need to accept them either.

For example, last summer a friend drove down to my rented Balboa Island beach house for a day. Our plan was to walk to the village for lunch, come back to my house, change clothes, grab the beach umbrella, and then luxuriate for the rest of the afternoon on the sand.

As we headed out the door for town, I dropped the house key in the back flap of my beach chair, which leans against the wall on the front porch. My friend paused and said, "Don't tell me you're leaving your house key there!"

"Yes, I am! I always pop it in that chair flap. That way I don't have to rummage around in my purse looking for it when I come home."

"Well," she said, "it doesn't seem wise or safe to me, but of course that's none of my business."

Finding her words mildly irritating but also thinking she might be right, I put the key in my shirt pocket instead of the chair flap. I also remembered why I only saw her a few times a year.

Finishing lunch and a very one-sided conversation where

I learned everything she had done, said, or thought in the last seven months, we returned home, changed clothes, and started for the beach. On the short walk there she said, "Now, you have your key, don't you?" Attempting to keep my claws retracted, I said, "Of course I have my key—it's in the flap of my beach chair!"

After another two hours of one-sided conversation, she announced how much she loved our chats but simply had to head for home. As we climbed the stairs to my front door, I attempted to find the house key in the back flap of my beach chair. In frustration I threw down the umbrella, pole, and all the other stuff in my hands and on my back to better free myself for the key search. (Wouldn't you think she could have carried something?)

"Don't tell me you've lost the key," my friend said.

Trying hard not to hiss, I said, "Of course I haven't lost the key; I transferred it from my pocket after lunch. I distinctly remember putting it here—just give me a minute."

"You obviously did not transfer that key; or it would be there!"

"I most certainly did transfer the key. Maybe it fell out on the sand." Rolling her eyes in exasperation, my friend trudged back with me to our "spot" to comb the sand with our fingers. No key. We walked back home.

A sweet guy painting a house across the street lugged his long ladder over to my second-story unit and insisted that he, not I, scamper up the ladder and walk through the open French doors (another safety infraction according to my friend) that led to the front entrance. As we walked in, I sheepishly thanked him and with relief saw my friend to her car. As she was driving away, her parting shot was, "Better call a locksmith, Marilyn, and then, for goodness' sake, take better care of your key!"

Pleased that I had not yielded to the instinct to claw her face, I ran up the stairs and down the hall. Grabbing the blouse I'd worn to lunch, I checked the pocket. There was my key! Contrary to my vehement insistence, I really had not transferred the key to my beach chair's flap. My friend was right. I hated that! She was overbearing, self-absorbed, and demeaning; she did not deserve to be right!

All evening I hoped she wouldn't phone to see if I'd called a locksmith. All evening I determined I would not admit to her that the key was in my pocket just as she had said it was. I even fabricated a great story about having returned to our sand spot where I met a wonderfully handsome, middle-aged man who compassionately helped me search through the sand and who found the key. We celebrated by having an intimate dinner later that evening. Carrying my fabrication even further, I imagined how he'd told me over dinner about the tragic death of his wife ten years ago and that I was the first woman he'd met since then who made him feel perhaps there was another love for him in the future. It was such a fun story, but of course I couldn't actually tell it to what's-her-face; after all, it was a complete and thoroughly compelling lie!

She called the next morning; I confessed. Her only comment was, "You really shouldn't live alone, Marilyn."

Meow!

. . . .

—*The Zippered Heart*

Honing Our Humor

● ● ● Barbara Johnson

God bought my life back from death, and I will continue to enjoy life.
—Job 33:28 NCV

*R*emember that just as you have different tastes in food and clothing, you have tastes in humor.

Know what kind of humor appeals to you, and look for it in films, videos, cartoons, books, and magazines. Also, seek out people who make you laugh. It may be a certain friend, or one of your children, or a grandchild. Whoever it is, spend time with that person.

Do everything you can to cultivate a sense of humor, which involves more than just telling jokes. A sense of humor is connected to the way you look at life, the way you can chuckle over what is absurd and ridiculous, the way you put your problems in perspective, and the way you can feel joy because you know that:

Any day above ground is a good one!

· ·

—*Daily Splashes of Joy*

Expect Delays

● ● ● Patsy Clairmont

I was en route to the airport when I spotted a flashing sign. Now, even though this is the same road I always travel and the roads have been under construction for many months, this was the first time I took note of the sign. Flashing in foot-high letters were these words: *Expect delays*.

Isn't that the truth? Everything is at least a little broken.

Systems, equipment, people skills, and routines cause holdups, postponements, and big fat delays.

Take grocery carts. I don't know why the one I take is always lame. It clatters so loudly that people stare and snarl at me like it's my fault. In fact, they act as though I brought it from home in this condition just to annoy them. The front wheel keeps jamming, which causes me to belly up to the cart and heave my weight against it just to keep it rolling. Then, when I go around a corner, I have to lift the whole back end (its, not mine) to maneuver around the end displays. What should have taken me fifteen minutes has now taken a chunk out of my morning . . . and I haven't even made it to the checkout line.

Expect delays.

Checkout lines were designed to find out if our conversion to Christianity was authentic. There, between the chewing gum and the plastic bags, as we stand next to the conveyor belt, impatience has an opportunity to bloom and flourish. It starts with the person in front of you, who seems to have purposed to pick up every product in the store that isn't priced. And price-check announcements over the PA system seem to be an indicator that all price-check personnel should go on break. By the time the price check is complete and the items are tallied, it now occurs to the purchaser that she actually has to pay for her groceries. That's when she goes in search of checkbooks, credit cards, or money. For women, that means digging into the recesses of their purses. Entire arms disappear into the folds of her bag, wagging about in search of the thirty-two cents it will take to bring financial closure. Fistfuls of debris emerge—gum wrappers, safety pins, and dusty peanuts—until, at last, the rusty coins hinged together with chewed Juicy Fruit are unearthed. By then I have begun to mutter phrases not printed in the New Testament.

Expect delays.

Recently, I flew from Detroit to Boston. Direct. What failed to join me was one of my suitcases, which was marked "Priority" by the airlines. How does one suitcase make it, but not the other one? And lucky me, it was the case that contained all my makeup and underwear—which when either are eliminated from my wardrobe causes seismic reactions. Trust me, I need both.

It wasn't like I went to Boston via Okinawa. C'mon, folks, it was a straight shot. When I reported my missing bag, the lady pushed her computer keys and then announced, "Good news; it's been found in Detroit." To which I quipped, "Well, I hope so, since that's the only place I've been."

Expect delays.

When the gentleman put up his hand to stop me from going through security at the airport, I complied. I already had stripped off my shoes, jacket, and purse to be scanned.

After an inordinate amount of time, the man waved me through and then immediately began wanding me. The wand sounded like a loaded Geiger counter that had just struck pay dirt as he whisked it around my chubby anatomy. The woman on the scanner then pointed out that my purse and carry-on needed to be searched.

I wondered what about me generated such interest. Was it my intimidating five-foot stature? I don't know, maybe a rash of elderly women had tried to slip their plastic tweezers through, and I fit the MO. Or maybe the security personnel thought it suspicious that I had enough snacks to feed the population of Nebraska.

Expect delays.

I bet the Israelites never anticipated that it would take them forty years to reach the Promised Land. Talk about delays. Enemies, rebellion, war, sickness . . . there was always something slowing them down and delaying their arrival.

What looked like sheer inconvenience and man-made barriers actually had been orchestrated by the hand of God. He knew the exact moment they would reach their destination. Delays were as much in His plan as manna and quails.

I remind myself of that when a flight is canceled, a mistake is made, an order is lost, a doctor's report is delayed, or a request is misunderstood. We don't know, but God might be protecting us with these delays. One thing I do know for certain: delays expose human frailty. So maybe we should take notes next time we're held up. It may be God's way of helping us realize our need for trust, patience, adaptability, and relinquishment.

Expect delays.

. . . .

—*All Cracked Up*

The Marriage Proposal

● ● ● Luci Swindoll

One of my friends at Women of Faith has an eighty-one-year-old grandmother who got a marriage proposal from her ninety-one-year-old "boyfriend." She can't decide whether or not to marry him . . . she wants to think about it. In the meantime, my friend suggested she hurry up before she's too old to be a flower girl. Don't you just *love* that?

....

—Life! Celebrate It

An Early Engagement

● ● ● Sheila Walsh

Although I never dated much, I do have a past. I was engaged at ten! Not many people can claim that on a resume. I didn't see it coming, so I was as surprised then as I'm sure you are now. There was a boy in my class at school whom I liked a lot. His name was Jim. I sat behind him and was fascinated by the way his dark hair curled on the collar of his school blazer. I had an overwhelming urge on a daily basis to touch his curly locks, but I was a good Baptist, so I suppressed my desire.

As Valentine's Day approached that year, I wondered if I dared send a card expressing my admiration for his brown eyes and his silken locks. My allowance did not provide for the kind of card that I wanted to give him, so I decided to make one. I took an empty Cornflakes box and cut it open to reveal the blank cardboard inside. I glued the rooster sides together so that I now had a clean slate on which to express myself.

There is something so full of possibility about a blank piece of paper. Before I committed to the first stroke of the paintbrush or the first word, it was perfect, full of promise, but sadly for me it was all downhill from that point on. In my head, I saw great beauty, but it never made it out onto the paper. So I remained the only one who knew of my potential to become a master painter or recipient of the Nobel Prize in Literature. All I can honestly say for that occasion is I did my best.

The following day was February the fourteenth, so I tucked the card inside my school bag. It was a cold, rainy day, as would be the norm between September and June of any given year on the west coast of Scotland. I crept into the classroom before the school bell rang and slipped the now-sodden card into Jim's desk. As my classmates began to file in, my heart was thumping in my chest. I panicked and considered removing the card before he saw it, but it was too late. I was sure he would laugh at me. I thought of all the extravagant, expensive cards that I had pored over in the drugstore. Some were so thickly padded they looked as if they had been made by a mattress company. My offering was pathetic. When the teacher asked us to open our desks and take out our workbooks, I almost fainted. Jim opened his desk, took out his book, and closed it again. How could he have missed my soggy card? Perhaps he saw it and was being kind enough to ignore it?

All day he said nothing. When the school bell rang at four o'clock, I headed home with a heavy heart. The following day, Jim approached me in the school yard before first bell and handed me a small package. I opened it, and inside was an engagement ring. It wasn't a toy or a cheap imitation; it was a gold band with three sapphires and two diamonds.

As you can imagine, I was shocked. I had no idea that one card could unlock such a floodgate. I asked him where he got it, and he informed me that he had found it on the beach one day and had been saving it for the right girl and the right moment.

He was not a man of many words; he simply looked at me and said, "This is it!"

My mother didn't see it that way, and that evening I had to take the ring to the police station and turn it in as lost property. After six months, the ring was unclaimed and returned to me so that my engagement period could continue. We smiled at each other at least twice a day, he put my name on his soccer ball, and I wrote his name inside my school bag in permanent ink, and that was the extent of our engagement.

. . . .

—*I'm Not Wonder Woman, But God Made Me Wonderful!*

Acknowledgments

Grateful acknowledgment is made to the publishers and copyright holders who granted permission to reprint copyrighted material.

Part 1 • *Can You Believe I Did That?*

"Tea Time and Supper" by Marilyn Meberg taken from *Contagious Joy*. Nashville: W Publishing, a Division of Thomas Nelson, 2006. All rights reserved.

"Fashion Non-Sense" taken from *I Think, Therefore I Have a Headache* by Martha Bolton. Grand Rapids: Bethany, a division of Baker, 2003.

"Celebrating Camaraderie" taken from *You Bring the Confetti* by Luci Swindoll. Nashville: W Publishing, a Division of Thomas Nelson, 1997. All rights reserved.

"In Search of a Giggle" taken from *All Cracked Up* by Patsy Clairmont. Nashville: W Publishing, a Division of Thomas Nelson, 2006. All rights reserved.

"Angerless Charade" taken from *I'm Not Wonder Woman* by Sheila Walsh. Nashville: Thomas Nelson, 2006. All rights reserved.

"Living in God's House" by Luci Swindoll taken from *Contagious Joy*. Nashville. W Publishing, a Division of Thomas Nelson, 2006. All rights reserved.

"Weighty Matters" taken from *All Cracked Up* by Patsy Clairmont. Nashville: W Publishing, a Division of Thomas Nelson, 2006. All rights reserved.

"We Are Relaxed" taken from *Choosing the Amusing* by Marilyn Meberg. Nashville: W Publishing, a Division of Thomas Nelson, 1999. All rights reserved.

Part 2 • *Laugh? I Thought I'd Die!*

"Putting on the Ritz" taken from *Silver in the Slop and Other Surprises* by Cathy Lee Phillips. Canton, GA: Patchwork Press, 2004. www.cathyleephillips.com. Used by permission. All rights reserved.

"Is This a Disaster—Or a Pimple-Level Problem?" taken from *Come Thirsty* by Max Lucado. Nashville: W Publishing, a Division of Thomas Nelson, 2004. All rights reserved.

"Cheer Up!" taken from *Daily Splashes of Joy* by Barbara Johnson. Nashville: W Publishing, a Division of Thomas Nelson, 2005. All rights reserved.

"Surviving All Those Aggravating A-teds" taken from *Listen Up, Honey: Good News for Your Soul!* by Thelma Wells. Nashville: W Publishing, a Division of Thomas Nelson, 2006. All rights reserved.

"Sharing Comfort in the Cesspool" taken from *Daily Splashes of Joy* by Barbara Johnson. Nashville: W Publishing, a Division of Thomas Nelson, 2005. All rights reserved.

"The Fun of Imperfection" taken from *Life in the Blender* by Sandi Patty. taken from *Daily Splashes of Joy* by Barbara Johnson. Nashville: W Publishing, a Division of Thomas Nelson, 2006. All rights reserved.

"If You're Happy and You Know It . . ." taken from *Listen Up, Honey: Good News for Your Soul!* by Thelma Wells. Nashville: W Publishing, a Division of Thomas Nelson, 2006. All rights reserved.

"Lord, Did You Misunderstand?" taken *The Real Me* by Natalie Grant. Nashville: W Publishing, a Division of Thomas Nelson, 2005. All rights reserved.

"Keep Your Joy, No Matter What" by Thelma Wells taken from *The Great Adventure*. Nashville: W Publishing, a Division of Thomas Nelson, 2002. All rights reserved.

"Filling Your Blessing Basket" by Sheila Walsh taken from *Contagious Joy*. Nashville: W Publishing, a Division of Thomas Nelson, 2006. All rights reserved.

"Finding Joy in a Cluttered-Up Sunset" taken from *Listen Up, Honey: Good News for Your Soul!* by Thelma Wells. Nashville: W Publishing, a Division of Thomas Nelson, 2006. All rights reserved.

"Family Adjustments" taken from *Life in the Blender* by Sandi Patty. Nashville: W Publishing, a Division of Thomas Nelson, 2006. All rights reserved.

"Back-Alley Laughter" taken from *Listen Up, Honey: Good News for Your Soul!* by Thelma Wells. Nashville: W Publishing, a Division of Thomas Nelson, 2006. All rights reserved.

"Look for the Laugh" by Barbara Johnson taken from *Contagious Joy*. Nashville: W Publishing, a Division of Thomas Nelson, 2006. All rights reserved.

"Being a Friend, Even When It Hurts" taken from *Big Girls Don't Whine* by Jan Silvious. Nashville: W Publishing, a Division of Thomas Nelson, 2003. All rights reserved.

"Bringing Your Pity Party to a Screeching Halt" by Thelma Wells taken from *The Great Adventure*. Nashville: W Publishing, a Division of Thomas Nelson, 2002. All rights reserved.

"God's E-mail" taken from *Freedom Inside and Out* by Marilyn Meberg. Nashville: W Publishing, a Division of Thomas Nelson, 2006. All rights reserved.

Part 3 • *Is This Funny, or Am I Losing My Mind?*

"Brain Fractures" taken from *All Cracked Up* by Patsy Clairmont. Nashville: W Publishing, a Division of Thomas Nelson, 2006. All rights reserved.

"The Limpings of the Well-Intended and Misinformed" by Marilyn Meberg taken from *Contagious Joy*. Nashville: W Publishing, a Division of Thomas Nelson, 2006. All rights reserved.

"If Only I Had a Brain . . ." by Ann Luna. Used by permission of Sue Ann Jones. All rights reserved.

"Are You the One?" taken from *Daily Splashes of Joy* by Barbara Johnson. Nashville: W Publishing, a Division of Thomas Nelson, 2005. All rights reserved.

"It's Gotta Be Here Somewhere" taken from *I Think, Therefore I Have a Headache* by Martha Bolton. Grand Rapids: Bethany, a division of Baker, 2003.

"Learning the Hard Way" taken from *Listen Up, Honey: Good News for Your Soul!* by Thelma Wells. Nashville: W Publishing, a Division of Thomas Nelson, 2006. All rights reserved.

"The Joyful Trickster" taken from *Choosing the Amusing* by Marilyn Meberg. Nashville: W Publishing, a Division of Thomas Nelson, 1999. All rights reserved.

"Doing and Being" taken from *Wide My World, Narrow My Bed* by Luci Swindoll. Nashville: W Publishing, a Division of Thomas Nelson, 1982. All rights reserved.

"My Little Chickadee" by Marilyn Meberg taken from *Irrepressible Hope*. Nashville: W Publishing, a Division of Thomas Nelson, 2003. All rights reserved.

"Cleaning Up after the Chaos" taken from *Life in the Blender* by Sandi Patty. Nashville: W Publishing, a Division of Thomas Nelson, 2006. All rights reserved.

"Are You Talking to Yourself Again?" taken from *Girl, Have I Got News for You* by Thelma Wells. Nashville: W Publishing, a Division of Thomas Nelson, 2004. All rights reserved.

"Pondering Backward" taken from *Life, Celebrate It!* by Luci Swindoll. Nashville: W Publishing, a Division of Thomas Nelson, 2006. All rights reserved.

Part 4 • *Family Funnies*

"The Big Day" taken from *Unexpected Grace* by Sheila Walsh. Nashville: Thomas Nelson, 2002.

"It's a Man Thang!" taken from *Girl, Have I Got News for You* by Thelma Wells. Nashville: W Publishing, a Division of Thomas Nelson, 2004. All rights reserved.

"Daddy Goes with Me" taken from *Life, Celebrate It!* by Luci Swindoll. Nashville: W Publishing, a Division of Thomas Nelson, 2006. All rights reserved.

"Brace for Impact!" taken from *Humor Me, I'm Your Mother* by Barbara Johnson. Nashville: W Publishing, a Division of Thomas Nelson, 2006. All rights reserved.

"God's Heart for His Girls" taken from *Big Girls Don't Whine* by Jan Silvious. Nashville: W Publishing, a Division of Thomas Nelson, 2003. All rights reserved.

"Don't Be Mad, Okay?" taken from *Nelson's Big Book of Laughter* by Lowell Streiker. Nashville: Thomas Nelson, 2000.

"Yahoo!" by Sheila Walsh taken from *Irrepressible Hope*. Nashville: W Publishing, a Division of Thomas Nelson, 2003. All rights reserved.

"God (and Uncle Bob) Bring Christmas" by Mary Graham taken from *Contagious Joy*. Nashville: W Publishing, a Division of Thomas Nelson, 2006. All rights reserved.

"A Little Too Much Time on the Road" taken from *Life in the Blender* by Sandi Patty. Nashville: W Publishing, a Division of Thomas Nelson, 2006. All rights reserved.

"A Sweet Reprieve from Cucumbers" taken from *Second Row, Piano Side* by Chonda Pierce. Kansas City, KS: Beacon Hill Press, 1996.

"Baby Doll" taken from *I Grew Up Little* by Patsy Clairmont. Nashville: W Publishing, a Division of Thomas Nelson, 2005. All rights reserved.

"I Know Where I'm Going" taken from *I'm Not Wonder Woman* by Sheila Walsh. Nashville: Thomas Nelson, 2006. All rights reserved.

"Mama T's Light-Bulb Moment" taken from *Listen Up, Honey: Good News for Your Soul!* by Thelma Wells. Nashville: W Publishing, a Division of Thomas Nelson, 2006. All rights reserved.

"Baby, It's Cold Inside!" taken from *All Cracked Up* by Patsy Clairmont. Nashville: W Publishing, a Division of Thomas Nelson, 2006. All rights reserved.

"Does This Thing Come with Directions?" taken from *I'm Not Wonder Woman* by Sheila Walsh. Nashville: Thomas Nelson, 2006. All rights reserved.

"Big-Girl Talk" taken from *Big Girls Don't Whine* by Jan Silvious. Nashville: W Publishing, a Division of Thomas Nelson, 2003. All rights reserved.

"If It's Important, Write It Down!" taken from *Life in the Blender* by Sandi Patty. Nashville: W Publishing, a Division of Thomas Nelson, 2006. All rights reserved.

Part 5 • *Healthy Hilarity*

"Regarding Food" taken from *Aging, Ailments, and Attitudes* by Cathy Lee Phillips. Canton, GA· Patchwork Press, 2003. www.cathyleephillips.com. Used by permission. All rights reserved.

"The Butcher's Scales" taken from *I'm Not Wonder Woman* by Sheila Walsh. Nashville: Thomas Nelson, 2006. All rights reserved.

"Fat Farm Failures" taken from *Living Somewhere Between Estrogen and Death* by Barbara Johnson. Nashville· W Publishing, a Division of Thomas Nelson, 1997. All rights reserved.

"Hundred-Dollar Ringworm" taken from *Since You Asked* by Marilyn Meberg. Nashville· W Publishing, a Division of Thomas Nelson, 2006. All rights reserved.

"Touchy about Being Touched" taken from *Humor Me, I'm Your Mother* by Barbara Johnson. Nashville: W Publishing, a Division of Thomas Nelson, 2006. All rights reserved.

"Laugh It Up" taken from *I Think, Therefore I Have a Headache* by Martha Bolton. "Grand Rapids· Bethany, a division of Baker, 2003.

"The Year We Had Head Lice" taken from *Life in the Blender* by Sandi Patty. Nashville: W Publishing, a Division of Thomas Nelson, 2006 All rights reserved.

"Guilty Pleasures" taken from *You Bring the Confetti* by Luci Swindoll. Nashville: W Publishing, a Division of Thomas Nelson, 1997. All rights reserved.

"The Perils of Exercise" taken from *Daily Splashes of Joy* by Barbara Johnson. Nashville: W Publishing, a Division of Thomas Nelson, 2005. All rights reserved.

"Nonsense in Their Veins" taken from *Life, Celebrate It!* by Luci Swindoll. Nashville. W Publishing, a Division of Thomas Nelson, 2006. All rights reserved.

"Find the Joy!" taken from *Life in the Blender* by Sandi Patty. Nashville: W Publishing, a Division of Thomas Nelson, 2006. All rights reserved.

"My Favorite Excuse" taken from *Daily Splashes of Joy* by Barbara Johnson. Nashville: W Publishing, a Division of Thomas Nelson, 2005. All rights reserved.

Part 6 • *Get Outta Here!*

"On an Olympic Scale, I'd Give It a 7.4" by Ann Luna. Used by permission of Sue Ann Jones. All rights reserved.

"Surprised by Doubt" taken from *Extraordinary Faith* by Sheila Walsh. Nashville: Thomas Nelson, 2005. All rights reserved.

"Climb In, Little Piggy?" taken from *Come Thirsty* by Max Lucado. Nashville: W Publishing, a Division of Thomas Nelson, 2004. All rights reserved.

"Spending Christmas with a Rodent" by Mary Graham taken from *Contagious Joy.* Nashville: W Publishing, a Division of Thomas Nelson, 2006. All rights reserved.

"Saving My Satin Pillows" taken from *Since You Asked* by Marilyn Meberg. Nashville: W Publishing, a Division of Thomas Nelson, 2006. All rights reserved.

"God's Garden" taken from *I Grew Up Little* by Patsy Clairmont. Nashville: W Publishing, a Division of Thomas Nelson, 2005. All rights reserved.

"Riding Shotgun with an Ex-Con Angel" by Ann Luna. Used by permission of Sue Ann Jones. All rights reserved.

"Public Speaking, Cesspool-Style" taken from *Living Somewhere Between Estrogen and Death* by Barbara Johnson. Nashville: W Publishing, a Division of Thomas Nelson, 1997. All rights reserved.

"Luci's Law" taken from *Notes to a Working Woman* by Luci Swindoll. Nashville: W Publishing, a Division of Thomas Nelson, 2005. All rights reserved.

"The Problems Started with the Birthday Cake" by Ann Luna. Used by permission of Sue Ann Jones. All rights reserved.

"Trying Not to Hiss" taken from *The Zippered Heart* by Marilyn Meberg. Nashville: W Publishing, a Division of Thomas Nelson, 2002. All rights reserved.

"Honing Our Humor" taken from *Daily Splashes of Joy* by Barbara Johnson. Nashville: W Publishing, a Division of Thomas Nelson, 2005. All rights reserved.

"Expect Delays taken from *All Cracked Up* by Patsy Clairmont. Nashville: W Publishing, a Division of Thomas Nelson, 2006. All rights reserved.

"The Marriage Proposal" taken from *Life, Celebrate It!* by Luci Swindoll. Nashville: W Publishing, a Division of Thomas Nelson, 2006. All rights reserved.

"An Early Engagement" taken from *I'm Not Wonder Woman* by Sheila Walsh. Nashville: Thomas Nelson, 2006. All rights reserved.